TEXAS LEGISLATIVE HANDBOOK ™

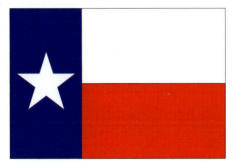

2015-2016
LEGISLATIVE ROSTER
WITH COMMITTEES
84th SESSION CONVENED:
JANUARY 13, 2015

Published by
Texas State Directory Press, Inc.
P.O. Box 12186, Austin, TX 78711-2186
512/477-5698   800/388-8075
FAX: 512/473-2447
http://www.txdirectory.com
Email: sdpress@txdirectory.com
ISBN: 978-0-934367-04-2

Copyright © 2015

Julie Sayers, Publisher/Editor

Thursday	January 1, 2015	New Year's Day*
Monday	January 19, 2015	Martin Luther King, Jr. Day*
Monday	January 19, 2015	Confederate Heroes' Day†
Monday	February 16, 2015	President's Day*
Monday	March 2, 2015	Texas Independence Day
Tuesday	March 31, 2015	Cesar Chavez Day**
Friday	April 3, 2015	Good Friday**
Tuesday	April 21, 2015	San Jacinto Day†
Monday	May 25, 2015	Memorial Day*
Friday	June 19, 2015	Emancipation Day†
Saturday	July 4, 2015	Independence Day*
Thursday	August 27, 2015	LBJ's Birthday†
Monday	September 7, 2015	Labor Day*
Monday	September 14, 2015	Rosh Hashanah**
Tuesday	September 15, 2015	Rosh Hashanah**
Wednesday	September 23, 2015	Yom Kippur
Wednesday	November 11, 2015	Veterans' Day*
Thursday	November 26, 2015	Thanksgiving Day*
Friday	November 27, 2015	Day After Thanksgiving*
Thursday	December 24, 2015	Christmas Eve*
Friday	December 25, 2015	Christmas Day*

Weekend Holidays: Offices will not be closed on another day when designated holidays fall on a Saturday or Sunday. Such holidays will not be observed.

† Skeleton Crew Holidays: Office must have enough employees to conduct business.

* National Holiday: All offices closed.

** Optional Holidays: Employee is entitled to observe Rosh Hashanah, Yom Kippur, Good Friday, and Cesar Chavez Day in lieu of any state holiday where a skeleton crew is required.

ADDRESSING PROCEDURES

To Write State Representatives:
The Honorable (full name)
Texas House of Representatives
P.O. Box 2910
Austin, TX 78768-2910
Dear Mr./Ms. (last name):

Speaking:
"Representative (last name)"
"Mr./Ms. (last name)"

Email:
Representatives:
firstname.lastname@house.state.tx.us

To Write State Senators:
The Honorable (full name)
Texas Senate
P.O. Box 12068
Austin, TX 78711-2068
Dear Senator (last name):

"Senator (last name)"

Senators:
firstname.lastname@senate.state.tx.us

STATEWIDE OFFICIALS

GOVERNOR GREG ABBOTT (R)

(Cecilia)

STATE CAPITOL
Room 2S.1
1100 Congress Avenue
Austin, TX 78701

v: 512/463-2000

Governor's Staff	Phone	Fax
Daniel Hodge, *Chief of Staff*	512/463-1762 /	463-5571
Kim Snyder, *Scheduling*	512/463-7210 /	475-2349
Stacey Napier, *Administration Director*	512/463-2000 /	463-8464
Luis Saenz, *Appointments Director*	512/463-1828 /	475-2576
Randy Erben, *Legislative Director*	512/463-1830 /	475-2211
Matt Hirsch, *Communications Director*	512/463-1826 /	463-1847
Amelia Chassé, *Press Secretary*	512/463-1826 /	463-1847
Kara Belew, *Budget Director*	512/463-1778 /	463-1975
Drew DeBerry, *Policy Director*	512/463-1778 /	463-1975
Jimmy Blacklock, *General Counsel*	512/463-1788 /	463-1932

**ATTORNEY GENERAL
KEN PAXTON** (R)
(Angela)

Price Daniel Sr. Bldg.
209 W. 14th St. 78701
v: 512/463.2191

**SECRETARY OF STATE
CARLOS H.
CASCOS** (R)
(Aurora)

State Capitol Bldg.
Room 1E.8 78701
v: 512/463.5770

**COMPTROLLER OF
PUBLIC ACCOUNTS
GLENN HEGAR** (R)
(Dara)

LBJ Office Bldg.
111 E. 17th St. 78774
v: 512/463.4444

**LAND COMMISSIONER
GEORGE P. BUSH** (R)
(Amanda)

Stephen F. Austin Bldg.
1700 N. Congress 78701
v: 512/463.5001

**AGRICULTURE COMMISSIONER
SID MILLER** (R)
(Debra)

Stephen F. Austin Bldg.
1700 N. Congress 78701
v: 512/463-1408

114TH UNITED STATES CONGRESS

TEXAS DELEGATION

U.S. SENATORS

	Washington, D.C. 20510	(202) Phone/FAX No.
John Cornyn-R (Sandy)	517 Hart Senate Bldg	224-2934 / 228-2856
Ted Cruz-R (Heidi)	455 Dirksen Senate Bldg	224-5922 / 228-0755

U.S. REPRESENTATIVES

District	Washington, D.C. 20515	(202) Phone/FAX No.
1-Louis Gohmert-R (Kathy)	2243 Rayburn HOB	225-3035 / 226-1230
2-Ted Poe-R (Carol)	2412 Rayburn HOB	225-6565 / 225-5547
3-Sam Johnson-R (Shirley)	2304 Rayburn HOB	225-4201 / 225-1485
4-John Ratcliffe-R (Michele)	325 Cannon HOB	225-6673 / 225-3332
5-Jeb Hensarling-R (Melissa)	2228 Rayburn HOB	225-3484 / 226-4888
6-Joe L. Barton-R	2107 Rayburn HOB	225-2002 / 225-3052
7-John Culberson-R (Belinda)	2372 Rayburn HOB	225-2571 / 225-4381
8-Kevin Brady-R (Cathy)	301 Cannon HOB	225-4901 / 225-5524
9-Al Green-D	2347 Rayburn HOB	225-7508 / 225-2947
10-Michael McCaul-R (Linda)	131 Cannon HOB	225-2401 / 225-5955
11-Mike Conaway-R (Suzanne)	2430 Rayburn HOB	225-3605 / 225-1783
12-Kay Granger-R	1026 Longworth HOB	225-5071 / 225-5683
13-William M. "Mac" Thornberry-R (Sally)	2208 Rayburn HOB	225-3706 / 225-3486
14-Randy Weber-R (Brenda)	510 Cannon HOB	225-2831 / 225-0271
15-Ruben Hinojosa-D (Marty)	2262 Rayburn HOB	225-2531 / 225-5688
16-Robert F. O'Rourke-D (Amy)	1330 Longworth HOB	225-4831 / 225-2016
17-Bill Flores-R (Gina)	1030 Longworth HOB	225-6105 / 225-0350
18-Sheila Jackson Lee-D (Elwyn)	2252 Rayburn HOB	225-3816 / 225-3317
19-Randy Neugebauer-R (Dana)	1424 Longworth HOB	225-4005 / 225-9615
20-Joaquin Castro-D (Anna)	212 Cannon HOB	225-3236 / 225-1915
21-Lamar Smith-R (Beth)	2409 Rayburn HOB	225-4236 / 225-8628
22-Pete Olson-R (Nancy)	2133 Rayburn HOB	225-5951 / 225-5241
23-Will Hurd-R	317 Cannon HOB	225-4511 / 225-2237
24-Kenny Marchant-R (Donna)	2313 Rayburn HOB	225-6605 / 225-0074
25-Roger Williams-R (Patty)	1323 Longworth HOB	225-9896 / 225-9692
26-Michael C. Burgess-R (Laura)	2336 Rayburn HOB	225-7772 / 225-2919
27-Blake Farenthold-R (Debbie)	1027 Longworth HOB	225-7742 / 226-1134
28-Henry Cuellar-D (Imelda)	2209 Rayburn HOB	225-1640 / 225-1641
29-Gene Green-D (Helen)	2470 Rayburn HOB.	225-1688 / 225-9903
30-Eddie Bernice Johnson-D	2468 Rayburn HOB	225-8885 / 226-1477
31-John R. Carter-R (Erika)	2110 Rayburn HOB	225-3864 / 225-5886
32-Pete Sessions-R (Karen)	2233 Rayburn HOB	225-2231 / 225-5878
33-Marc Veasey-D (Tonya)	414 Cannon HOB	225-9897 / 225-9702
34-Filemon Vela-D (Rose)	437 Cannon HOB	225-9901 / 225-9770
35-Lloyd Doggett-D (Libby)	2307 Rayburn HOB	225-4865 / 225-3073
36-Brian Babin-R (Roxanne)	316 Cannon HOB	225-1555 / 226-0396

TEXAS SENATE

LIEUTENANT GOVERNOR
DAN PATRICK (R)

(Jan)

STATE CAPITOL
Room 2E.13
1100 Congress Avenue
Austin, TX 78701

v: 512/463-0001
f: 512/463-8668

Lieutenant Governor's Staff

Logan Spence, *Chief of Staff* 512/463-0001
Walter Fisher, *Senior Advisor* 512/463-2998
Colby Beuck, *Legislative Coordinator* 512/463-4088
Hannah Hamilton, *Scheduler* 512/463-2212
Keith Elkins, *Dir. of Communications* 512/463-8186
Karina Casari Davis, *Parliamentarian* 512/463-0248
Mike Morrissey, *Budget Director* 512/463-3860
Kate McGrath, *Policy Director* 512/463-2525
Darrell Davila, *General Counsel* 512/463-0295

Senate Staff

Patsy Spaw, *Secretary of the Senate* 512/463-0100
Tracy Ortiz, *Calendar Clerk* 512/463-0060
Scott Caffey, *Committee Coordinator* 512/463-0070
Patience Worrel, *Enrolling Clerk* 512/463-0321
Polly Emerson, *Journal Clerk* 512/463-0050
Rick DeLeon, *Sergeant-at-Arms* 512/463-0200

SENATE MEMBERS BY DISTRICT

1 †Eltife (R)	9 †Hancock (R)	17 †Huffman (R)	25 †Campbell (R)
2 Hall (R)	10 Burton (R)	18 Kolkhorst (R)	26 Menéndez (D)
3 †Nichols (R)	11 †Taylor, L (R)	19 †Uresti (D)	27 †Lucio (D)
4 Creighton (R)	12 †Nelson (R)	20 †Hinojosa (D)	28 Perry (R)
5 †Schwertner (R)	13 †Ellis (D)	21 †Zaffirini (D)	29 †Rodríguez (D)
6 †Garcia (D)	14 †Watson (D)	22 †Birdwell (R)	30 †Estes (R)
7 Bettencourt (R)	15 †Whitmire (D)	23 †West (D)	31 †Seliger (R)
8 Taylor, V. (R)	16 Huffines (R)	24 †Fraser (R)	

†Incumbent

SENATORS

PAUL BETTENCOURT (R)

(Susan) **Houston**
Dist. 7 - Harris (20%)

CAPITOL OFFICE
v: 512/463-0107
f: 512/463-8810
E1.712

Staff: VA Stephens
Brad Tegeler

Intergovernmental Relations (VC); Education; Finance; Higher Education

BIRDWELL, BRIAN (R)

(Mel) **Granbury**

Dist. 22 - Bosque, Ellis, Falls, Hill, Hood, Johnson, McLennan, Navarro, Somervell, Tarrant (5%)

*Nominations (C); Natural Resources and Economic Dev.; State Affairs; Veterans Affairs & Mil. Installations, **Subcomm. on Border Security (C)***

CAPITOL OFFICE

v: 512/463-0122
f: 512/475-3729
E1.706

Staff: Ben Stratmann
Anna Paulson
Liz Sanchez

BURTON, KONNI (R)

(Phil) **Colleyville**

Dist. 10 - Tarrant (46%)

Veterans Affairs & Military Installations (VC); Criminal Justice; Higher Education; Nominations

CAPITOL OFFICE

v: 512/463-0110
f: 512/475-3745
GE.7

Staff: Art Martinez
Tyler Norris
Cathy Scott

CAMPBELL, M.D., DONNA (R)

(Stan) **New Braunfels**

Dist. 25 - Bexar (24%), Comal, Guadalupe (62%), Hays (69%), Kendall, Travis (7%)

Veterans Affairs & Military Installations (C); Administration; Education; Health & Human Services; Intergovernmental Relations

CAPITOL OFFICE

v: 512/463-0125
f: 512/463-7794
3E.8

Staff: Stephanie Matthews
Jon Oliver

CREIGHTON, BRANDON (R)

(Fawn) **Conroe**

Dist. 4 - Chambers, Galveston (1%), Harris (3%), Jefferson, Montgomery (86%)

Business & Commerce (VC); Agriculture, Water and Rural Affairs; Criminal Justice; State Affairs

CAPITOL OFFICE

v: 512/463-0104
f: 512/463-6373
E1.606

Staff: Tara Garcia
Adrianne Evans
Eliza Vielma

ELLIS, RODNEY (D)

(Licia) **Houston**

Dist. 13 - Fort Bend (19%), Harris (17%)

State Affairs (VC); Business & Commerce; Transportation

CAPITOL OFFICE

v: 512/463-0113
f: 512/463-0006
3E.6

Staff: Brandon Dudley
David Edmonson
Jessica Schleifer

ELTIFE, KEVIN P. (R)

(Kelly) **Tyler**

Dist. 1 - Bowie, Camp, Cass, Franklin, Gregg, Harrison, Lamar, Marion, Morris, Panola, Red River, Rusk, Smith, Titus, Upshur, Wood

Business & Commerce (C); Administration; Finance

CAPITOL OFFICE

v: 512/463-0101
f: 512/475-3751
3E.16

Staff: Cheryl Vanek
Connie Hernandez
Ryan Weiseman

ESTES, CRAIG (R)

(Jennifer) **Wichita Falls**

Dist. 30 - Archer, Clay, Collin (15%), Cooke, Denton (17%), Erath, Grayson, Jack, Montague, Palo Pinto, Parker, Wichita, Wise, Young

Natural Resources and Economic Development (VC); Health & Human Services; Nominations; State Affairs

CAPITOL OFFICE

v: 512/463-0130
f: 512/463-8874
3E.18

Staff: Noe Barrios
Katherine Metcalf

FRASER, TROY (R)

(Linda) **Horseshoe Bay**

Dist. 24 - Bandera, Bell, Blanco, Brown, Burnet, Callahan, Comanche, Coryell, Gillespie, Hamilton, Kerr, Lampasas, Llano, Mills, San Saba, Taylor (70%), Travis (5%)

Natural Resources and Economic Development (C); Nominations; State Affairs; Transportation

CAPITOL OFFICE

v: 512/463-0124
f: 512/475-3732
1E.12

Staff: Terri Mathis
Will McAdams

GARCIA, SYLVIA R. (D)

Houston

Dist. 6 - Harris (20%)

Education; Intergovernmental Relations; Transportation; Veterans Affairs & Military Installations

CAPITOL OFFICE

v: 512/463-0106
f: 512/463-0346
3E.12

Staff: Sara Gonzalez
Perla Cavazos

HALL, BOB (R)

(Kay) **Edgewood**

Dist. 2 - Dallas (17%), Delta, Fannin, Hopkins, Hunt, Kaufman, Rains, Rockwall, Van Zandt

Veterans Affairs & Military Installations, SC on Border Security (VC); Agriculture, Water and Rural Affairs; Natural Resources and Economic Development; Transportation

CAPITOL OFFICE

v: 512/463-0102
f: 512/463-7202
E1.808

Staff: Amy Lane
Boyd Bush
Drinda Randall

HANCOCK, KELLY G. (R)

(Robin) **North Richland Hills**

Dist. 9 - Dallas (9%), Tarrant (34%)

Administration (C); Finance; Natural Resources and Economic Development; Transportation

CAPITOL OFFICE

v: 512/463-0109
f: 512/463-7003
1E.9

Staff: Tricia Stinson
Adam Leggett

HINOJOSA, JUAN "CHUY" (D)

McAllen

Dist. 20 - Brooks, Hidalgo (58%), Jim Wells, Nueces (99%)

Finance (VC); Agriculture, Water and Rural Affairs; Criminal Justice; Natural Resources and Economic Development

CAPITOL OFFICE

v: 512/463-0120
f: 512/463-0229
3E.10

Staff: Luis Moreno
Jennifer Saenz

HUFFINES, DON (R)

(Mary Catherine) **Dallas**

Dist. 16 - Dallas (34%)

Transportation (VC); Administration; Business & Commerce; Education

CAPITOL OFFICE

v: 512/463-0116
f: 512/463-3135
E1.608

Staff: Matt Langston
Brent Connett
Chris McNutt

HUFFMAN, JOAN (R)

(Keith) **Houston**

Dist. 17 - Brazoria (31%), Fort Bend (32%), Harris (13%)

State Affairs (C); Criminal Justice (VC); Finance

CAPITOL OFFICE

v: 512/463-0117
f: 512/463-0639
1E.15

Staff: Wroe Jackson
Amanda Jenson

KOLKHORST, LOIS W. (R)

(Jim) **Brenham**

Dist. 18 - Aransas, Austin, Burleson, Calhoun, Colorado, DeWitt, Fayette, Fort Bend (49%), Goliad, Gonzales, Harris (1%), Jackson, Lavaca, Lee, Matagorda, Nueces (1%), Refugio, Victoria, Waller, Washington, Wharton

Health & Human Services (VC); Agriculture, Water and Rural Affairs; Education; Finance; Transportation

CAPITOL OFFICE

v: 512/463-0118
f: 512/475-3736
3E.2

Staff: Chris Steinbach
Ross Giesinger
Matthew Russell
Cheryl Tiemann

LUCIO, JR., EDDIE (D)

(Minnie) **Brownsville**

Dist. 27 - Cameron, Hidalgo (42%), Kenedy, Kleberg, Willacy

Intergovernmental Relations (C); Education (VC); Natural Res. and Eco. Dev.;Veterans Affairs & Military Instal.,Subcomm. on Border Security

CAPITOL OFFICE

v: 512/463-0127
f: 512/463-0061
3S.5

Staff: Louie Sanchez
Daniel Esparza

MENÉNDEZ, JOSÉ (D)

(Nicole) **San Antonio**

Dist. 26 - Bexar (47%)

Criminal Justice; Higher Education; Intergovernmental Relations

CAPITOL OFFICE

v: 512/463-0126
f: 512/463-2114
3S.3

Staff: Dwight Clark
Judy Peterson
Jeff Peterson

NELSON, JANE (R)

(J. Michael) **Flower Mound**

Dist. 12 - Denton (83%), Tarrant (15%)

Finance (C); State Affairs

CAPITOL OFFICE

v: 512/463-0112
f: 512/463-0923
1E.5

Staff: Dave Nelson
Megan Hanson
Elizabeth Rice

NICHOLS, ROBERT (R)

(Donna) **Jacksonville**

Dist. 3 - Anderson, Angelina, Cherokee, Hardin, Henderson, Houston, Jasper, Liberty, Montgomery (14%), Nacogdoches, Newton, Orange, Polk, Sabine, San Augustine, San Jacinto, Shelby, Trinity, Tyler

Transportation (C); Finance; Intergovernmental Relations; Natural Resources and Economic Development

CAPITOL OFFICE

v: 512/463-0103
f: 512/463-1526
E1.704

Staff: Angus Lupton
Sydni Mitchell
J.D. Hale

PERRY, CHARLES (R)

(Jacklyn) **Lubbock**

Dist. 28 - Baylor, Borden, Childress, Coke, Coleman, Concho, Cottle, Crane, Crosby, Dawson, Dickens, Eastland, Fisher, Floyd, Foard, Garza, Hale, Hardeman, Haskell, Hockley, Irion, Jones, Kent, Kimble, King, Knox, Lamb, Lubbock, Lynn, Mason, McCulloch, Menard, Mitchell, Motley, Nolan, Reagan, Runnels, Schleicher, Scurry, Shackelford, Stephens, Sterling, Stonewall, Sutton, Taylor (30%), Terry, Throckmorton, Tom Green, Upton, Ward, Wilbarger

Agriculture, Water and Rural Affairs (C); Criminal Justice; Health & Human Services; Higher Education

CAPITOL OFFICE

v: 512/463-0128
f: 512/463-2424
E1.810

Staff: Scott Hutchinson
Matthew Dowling
Shannon Harmon

RODRÍGUEZ, JOSÈ R. (D)

(Carmen) **El Paso**

Dist. 29 - Culberson, El Paso, Hudspeth, Jeff Davis, Presidio

Agriculture, Water and Rural Affairs; Education; Health & Human Services; Nominations; Veterans Affairs & Military Installations

CAPITOL OFFICE

v: 512/463-0129
f: 512/463-7100
E1.610

Staff: Sushma Smith
Sito Negron
Allison Brooks

SCHWERTNER, M.D., CHARLES (R)

(Belinda) **Georgetown**

Dist. 5 - Brazos, Freestone, Grimes, Leon, Limestone, Madison, Milam, Robertson, Walker, Williamson

Health & Human Services (C); Administration; Business & Commerce; Finance; State Affairs

CAPITOL OFFICE

v: 512/463-0105
f: 512/463-5713
E1.806

Staff: Tom Holloway
Leah Alexander
Nelson Jarrin

SELIGER, KEL (R)

(Nancy) **Amarillo**

Dist. 31 -Andrews, Armstrong, Bailey, Briscoe, Carson, Castro, Cochran, Collingsworth, Dallam, Deaf Smith, Donley, Ector, Gaines, Glasscock, Gray, Hall, Hansford, Hartley, Hemphill, Howard, Hutchinson, Lipscomb, Loving, Martin, Midland, Moore, Ochiltree, Oldham, Parmer, Potter, Randall, Roberts, Sherman, Swisher, Wheeler, Winkler, Yoakum

Higher Education (C); Business & Commerce; Education; Finance; Natural Resources and Economic Development

CAPITOL OFFICE

v: 512/463-0131
f: 512/475-3733
GE.4

Staff: Ginger Averitt
Becky Womack
Tien Do

TAYLOR, LARRY (R)

(Kerri) **Friendswood**

Dist. 11 - Brazoria (69%),

Galveston (99%), Harris (7%)

Education (C); Business & Commerce; Finance; Intergovernmental Relations

CAPITOL OFFICE

v: 512/463-0111
f: 512/475-3727
GE.5

Staff: Cari Christman
Chris Noonan
Haley Cornyn

TAYLOR, VAN (R)

(Anne) **Plano**

Dist. 8 - Collin (85%), Dallas (5%)

Nominations (VC); Education; Health & Human Services; Transportation

CAPITOL OFFICE

v: 512/463-0108
f: 512/463-7579
E1.708

Staff: Lonnie Dietz
Jeremy Mazur
Sable Coleman

URESTI, CARLOS I. (D)

(Lleanna) **San Antonio**

Dist. 19 - Atascosa (98%), Bexar (29%), Brewster, Crockett, Dimmit, Edwards, Frio, Kinney, Maverick, Medina, Pecos, Real, Reeves, Terrell, Uvalde, Val Verde, Zavala

Administration (VC); Finance; Health & Human Services; Natural Resources and Economic Development

CAPITOL OFFICE

v: 512/463-0119
f: 512/463-1017
4E.2

Staff: Jason Hassay
Michael Ruggieri
Bryant Villa

WATSON, KIRK (D)

(Liz) **Austin**

Dist. 14 - Bastrop, Travis (74%)

Business & Commerce; Finance; Higher Education; Nominations

CAPITOL OFFICE

v: 512/463-0114
f: 512/463-5949
E1.804

Staff: Sarah Howard
Sandy Guzman
Kate Alexander

WEST, ROYCE (D)

(Carol) **Dallas**

Dist. 23 - Dallas (34%)

Higher Education (VC); Administration; Education; Finance

CAPITOL OFFICE

v: 512/463-0123
f: 512/463-0299
1E.3

Staff: LaJuana Barton
Graham Keever

WHITMIRE, JOHN (D)

Houston

Dist. 15 - Harris (19%)

Criminal Justice (C); Business & Commerce; Finance

CAPITOL OFFICE

v: 512/463-0115
f: 512/475-3737
1E.13

Staff: Lara Wendler
Trey Owens
Susan Fontenette

ZAFFIRINI, JUDITH (D)

(Carlos) **Laredo**

Dist. 21 - Atascosa (2%), Bee, Bexar (1%), Caldwell, Duval, Guadalupe (38%), Hays (31%), Jim Hogg, Karnes, LaSalle, Live Oak, McMullen, San Patricio, Starr, Travis (14%), Webb, Wilson, Zapata

Agriculture, Water and Rural Affairs (VC); Health & Human Services; Natural Resources and Economic Development; State Affairs

CAPITOL OFFICE

v: 512/463-0121
f: 512/475-3738
1E.14

Staff: Sean Griffin

SENATE STANDING COMMITTEES

Dan Patrick, *President of the Senate*   Juan Hinojosa, *President Pro Tem*

ADMINISTRATION
Clerk: Whitney Broughton   E1.714 • 512/463-0350 / Fax: 463-*0499*
Hancock, *Chair*   Uresti, *Vice Chair*

Members: Campbell, Eltife, Huffines, Schwertner, West

AGRICULTURE, WATER AND RURAL AFFAIRS
Clerk: Jeremy Hagen   335 Sam Houston Bldg • 512/463-0340 / Fax: 463-*2293*
Perry, *Chair*   Zaffirini, *Vice Chair*

Members: Creighton, Hall, Hinojosa, Kolkhorst, Rodríguez

BUSINESS & COMMERCE
Clerk: Brady Faglier 370 Sam Houston Bldg. • 512/463-0365 / Fax: 463-1613
Eltife, *Chair*   Creighton, *Vice Chair*

Members: Ellis, Huffines, Schwertner, Seliger, L. Taylor, Watson, Whitmire

CRIMINAL JUSTICE
Clerk: Jessica Cox   470 Sam Houston Bldg. • 512/463-0345 / Fax: 475-2015
Whitmire, *Chair*   Huffman, *Vice Chair*

Members: Burton, Creighton, Hinojosa, Menéndez, Perry,

EDUCATION
Clerk: Holly McCoy   440 Sam Houston Bldg. • 512/463-0355 / Fax: 463-7467
L. Taylor, *Chair*   Lucio, *Vice Chair*

Members: Bettencourt, Campbell, Garcia, Huffines, Kolkhorst, Rodríguez,
              Seliger, V. Taylor, West

FINANCE
Clerk: Stephanie Hoover E1.038 • 512463-0370 / Fax: 463-5752
Nelson, *Chair*   Hinojosa, *Vice Chair*

Members: Bettencourt, Eltife, Hancock, Huffman, Kolkhorst, Nichols,
              Schwertner, Seliger, L. Taylor, Uresti, Watson, West, Whitmire

SENATE STANDING COMMITTEES

HEALTH & HUMAN SERVICES
Clerk: Meagan Kirby   420 Sam Houston Bldg. • 512/463-0360 / Fax: 463-9889

Schwertner, *Chair* Kolkhorst, *Vice Chair*

Members: Campbell, Estes, Perry, Rodríguez, V. Taylor, Uresti, Zaffirini

HIGHER EDUCATION
Clerk: Sarah Harrington 320 Sam Houston Bldg. • 512/463-4788 / Fax: 463-0695

Seliger, *Chair*   West, *Vice Chair*

Members: Bettencourt, Burton, Menéndez, Perry, Watson

INTERGOVERNMENTAL RELATIONS
Clerk: Donna Chattham 475 Sam Houston Bldg. • 512/463-2527 / Fax: 463-2858

Lucio, *Chair*   Bettencourt, *Vice Chair*

Members: Campbell, Garcia, Menéndez, Nichols, L.Taylor

NATURAL RESOURCES AND ECONOMIC DEVELOPMENT
Clerk: Tatum Reagan   325 Sam Houston Bldg. • 512/463-0390 / Fax: 463-6769

Fraser, *Chair*   Estes, *Vice Chair*

Members: Birdwell, Hall, Hancock, Hinojosa, Lucio, Nichols, Seliger, Uresti, Zaffirini

NOMINATIONS
Clerk: Robert Haley   E1.716 • 512/463-2084 / Fax: 463-8123

Birdwell, *Chair*   V. Taylor, *Vice Chair*

Members: Burton, Estes, Fraser, Rodríguez, Watson

STATE AFFAIRS
Clerk: Ashley Brooks   380 Sam Houston Bldg. • 512/463-0380 / Fax: 463-0342

Huffman, *Chair*   Ellis, *Vice Chair*

Members: Birdwell, Creighton, Estes, Fraser, Nelson, Schwertner, Zaffirini

SENATE STANDING COMMITTEES

TRANSPORTATION
Clerk: Amy Jeter   450 Sam Houston Bldg. • 512/463-0067 / Fax: 463-0097

Nichols, *Chair*   Huffines, *Vice Chair*

Members: Ellis, Fraser, Garcia, Hall, Hancock, Kolkhorst, V. Taylor

VETERANS AFFAIRS & MILITARY INSTALLATIONS
Clerk: 345 Sam Houston Bldg. • 512/463-2211 / Fax: 463-7683

Campbell, *Chair*   Burton, *Vice Chair*

Members: Birdwell, Garcia, Hall, Lucio, Rodríguez

Subcommittee on Border Security
Clerk: 345 Sam Houston Bldg. • 512/463-2211 / Fax: 463-7683

Birdwell, *Chair*   Hall, *Vice Chair*

Member: Lucio

SENATE SEATING CHART

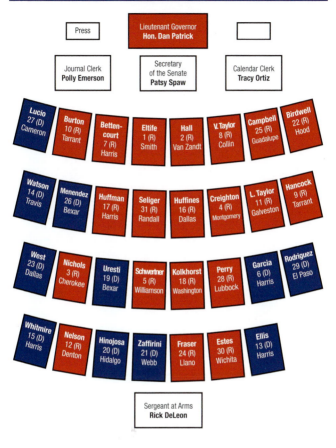

| Press | Lieutenant Governor **Hon. Dan Patrick** | |

| Journal Clerk **Polly Emerson** | Secretary of the Senate **Patsy Spaw** | Calendar Clerk **Tracy Ortiz** |

Lucio 27 (D) Cameron
Burton 10 (R) Tarrant
Bettencourt 7 (R) Harris
Eltife 1 (R) Smith
Hall 2 (R) Van Zandt
V. Taylor 8 (R) Collin
Campbell 25 (R) Guadalupe
Birdwell 22 (R) Hood

Watson 14 (D) Travis
Menendez 26 (D) Bexar
Huffman 17 (R) Harris
Seliger 31 (R) Randall
Huffines 16 (R) Dallas
Creighton 4 (R) Montgomery
L. Taylor 11 (R) Galveston
Hancock 9 (R) Tarrant

West 23 (D) Dallas
Nichols 3 (R) Cherokee
Uresti 19 (D) Bexar
Schwertner 5 (R) Williamson
Kolkhorst 18 (R) Washington
Perry 28 (R) Lubbock
Garcia 6 (D) Harris
Rodriguez 29 (D) El Paso

Whitmire 15 (D) Harris
Nelson 12 (R) Denton
Hinojosa 20 (D) Hidalgo
Zaffirini 21 (D) Webb
Fraser 24 (R) Llano
Estes 30 (R) Wichita
Ellis 13 (D) Harris

| Sergeant at Arms **Rick DeLeon** |

SENATE SENIORITY LEADERS

Member	No. of Years	No. of Sessions	
John Whitmire (D)	34	17	68th (1983)-84th Session
Judith Zaffirini (D)	30	15	70th (1987)-84th Session
Rodney Ellis (D)	28	14	71st (1990)-84th Session
Eddie Lucio (D)	26	13	72nd (1991)-84th Session
Jane Nelson (R)	24	12	73rd (1993)-84th Session
Royce West (D)	24	12	73rd (1993)-84th Session

#	Member	#	Member	#	Member
1	VanDeaver (R)	51	†Rodriguez, E. (D)	101	†Turner, C. (D)
2	†Flynn (R)	52	†Gonzales (R)	102	Koop (R)
3	†Bell (R)	53	Murr (R)	103	†Anchia (D)
4	Spitzer (R)	54	†Aycock (R)	104	†Alonzo (D)
5	†Hughes (R)	55	White, M. (R)	105	†Anderson, R. (R)
6	†Schaefer (R)	56	†Anderson, C. (R)	106	†Fallon (R)
7	†Simpson (R)	57	†Ashby (R)	107	†Sheets (R)
8	†Cook (R)	58	Burns (R)	108	Meyer (R)
9	†Paddie (R)	59	†Sheffield (R)	109	†Giddings (D)
10	Wray (R)	60	†Keffer (R)	110	†Rose (D)
11	†Clardy (R)	61	†King. P. (R)	111	†Davis, Y. (D)
12	†Kacal (R)	62	†Phillips (R)	112	†Button (R)
13	Schubert (R)	63	†Parker (R)	113	†Burkett (R)
14	†Raney (R)	64	†Crownover (R)	114	†Villalba (R)
15	Keough (R)	65	†Simmons (R)	115	Rinaldi (R)
16	Metcalf (R)	66	Shaheen (R)	116	†Martinez Fischer (D)
17	Cyrier (R)	67	†Leach (R)	117	Galindo (R)
18	†Otto (R)	68	†Springer (R)	118	†Farias (D)
19	White, J. (R)	69	†Frank (R)	119	†Gutierrez (D)
20	†Farney (R)	70	†Sanford (R)	120	†McClendon (D)
21	Phelan (R)	71	†King, S. (R)	121	†Straus (R)
22	†Deshotel (D)	72	†Darby (R)	122	†Larson (R)
23	Faircloth (R)	73	†Miller, D. (R)	123	Bernal (D)
24	†Bonnen, G. (R)	74	†Nevarez (D)	124	Pending
25	†Bonnen, D. (R)	75	†González (D)	125	†Rodriguez, J. (D)
26	†Miller, R. (R)	76	Blanco (D)	126	†Harless (R)
27	†Reynolds (D)	77	†Márquez (D)	127	†Huberty (R)
28	†Zerwas (R)	78	†Moody (D)	128	†Smith (R)
29	†Thompson, E. (R)	79	†Pickett (D)	129	Paul (R)
30	†Morrison (R)	80	†King, T. (D)	130	†Fletcher (R)
31	†Guillen (D)	81	Landgraf (R)	131	†Allen (D)
32	†Hunter (R)	82	†Craddick (R)	132	Schofield (R)
33	†Turner, Scott (R)	83	Burrows (R)	133	†Murphy (R)
34	†Herrero (D)	84	†Frullo (R)	134	†Davis, S. (R)
35	†Longoria (D)	85	†Stephenson (R)	135	†Elkins (R)
36	†Muñoz (D)	86	†Smithee (R)	136	†Dale (R)
37	†Oliveira (D)	87	†Price (R)	137	†Wu (D)
38	†Lucio (D)	88	†King, K. (R)	138	†Bohac (R)
39	†Martinez (D)	89	†Laubenberg (R)	139	†Turner, Sylvester (D)
40	†Canales (D)	90	Romero (D)	140	†Walle (D)
41	†Guerra (D)	91	†Klick (R)	141	†Thompson, S. (D)
42	†Raymond (D)	92	†Stickland (R)	142	†Dutton (D)
43	†Lozano (R)	93	†Krause (R)	143	†Hernandez (D)
44	†Kuempel (R)	94	Tinderholt (R)	144	Pena (R)
45	†Isaac (R)	95	†Collier (D)	145	†Alvarado (D)
46	†Dukes (D)	96	†Zedler (R)	146	†Miles (D)
47	†Workman (R)	97	†Goldman (R)	147	†Coleman (D)
48	†Howard (D)	98	†Capriglione (R)	148	†Farrar (D)
49	†Naishtat (D)	99	†Geren (R)	149	†Vo (D)
50	†Israel (D)	100	†Johnson (D)	150	†Riddle (R)

†Incumbent   (D) Democrat   (R) Republican

SPEAKER OF THE HOUSE
JOE STRAUS, III (R)

(Julie)

STATE CAPITOL
Room 2W.13
1100 Congress Avenue
Austin, TX 78701

v: 512/463-1000
f: 512/463-0675

Speaker's Staff

Jesse Ancira, *Chief of Staff* . . . . .512/463-0056 / 463-0675
Carolyn Scott, *Executive Assistant* . . . . .512/463-3000 / 463-0675
Tara Korstad, *Scheduler* . . . . .512/463-3000 / 463-0675
Patricia Shipton, *Strategic Legislative Advisor* . . . . .512/463-0056 / 463-0675
Andrew Blifford, *Budget Director* . . . . .512/463-1100 / 463-0278
Frank Battle, *Gen. Counsel and House Ethics Advisor* . . .512/463-1000 / 463-0278
Jason Embry, *Press Secretary* . . . . .512/463-0223 / 463-0675
Erin Daly Wilson, *Dir.of Appointments & Special Prog.* . . .512/463-1000 / 463-0675
Naomi Miller, *District Director* . . . . .210/828-4411 / 832-9994

House Staff

Steven Adrian, *Executive Director* . . . . .512/463-0835 / 463-0747
Robert Haney, *Chief Clerk* . . . . .512/463-0845 / 463-5896
Jennifer Doran , *Journal Clerk* . . . . .512/463-0855 / 463-2111
Chris Griesel, *House Parliamentarian* . . . . .512/463-2003 / 463-0153
Rod Welsh, *Sergeant-at-Arms* . . . . .512/463-0910 / 463-5896
Stacey Nicchio, *Committee Coordinator* . . . . .512/463-0850 / 463-7547
Mike Blackwell, *Communications-Video/Audio* . . . . .512/463-0920 / 463-5729
James Freeman, *Payroll-Personnel* . . . . .512/463-0865 / 463-8132

IMPORTANT LEGISLATIVE DATES

Friday, March 13, 2015 *(60th day)*	Deadline for filing bills and joint resolutions other than local bills, emergency appropriations and bills that have been declared an emergency by the governor.
Monday, June 1, 2015 *(140th day)* **Regular Session Ends**	Last day of the 84th Regular Session; corrections only in house and senate.
Sunday, June 21, 2015 *(20th day following final adjournment)*	Last day governor can sign or veto bills passed during the regular legislative session.
Monday, August 31, 2015 *(91st day following final adjournment)*	Date that bills without specific effective dates (that could not be effective immediately) become law

ALLEN, ALMA A. (D)

Houston
Dist. 131 - Harris (4%)
Sens. Ellis, Garcia, Huffman

Public Education (VC); Corrections; House Administration

CAPITOL OFFICE
v: 512/463-0744
f: 512/463-0761
E1.506

Staff: Anneliese Vogel
Dr. Teresa Lenoir
Wilma Jordan

ALONZO, ROBERTO R. (D)

(Sylvana) **Dallas**
Dist. 104 - Dallas (7%)
Sens. Hancock, West

Pensions (VC); Calendars; Higher Education; House Administration

CAPITOL OFFICE
v: 512/463-0408
f: 512/463-1817
1N.12

Staff: Jesse R. Bernal
Jerome Garza

ALVARADO, CAROL (D)

Houston
Dist. 145 - Harris (4%)
Sens. Ellis, Garcia, L. Taylor, Whitmire

Urban Affairs (C); Special Purpose Districts (VC); Rules & Resolutions

CAPITOL OFFICE
v: 512/463-0732
f: 512/463-4781
E2.808

Staff: Crystal Ford
Alexander Hammond
Bettina Olivares

ANCHIA, RAFAEL (D)

(Marissa) **Dallas**
Dist. 103 - Dallas (7%)
Sens. Hancock, Huffines, West

International Trade & Intergovernmental Affairs (C); Energy Resources

CAPITOL OFFICE
v: 512/463-0746
f: 512/463-5896
4N.6

Staff: Liz Zornes
Tricia Horatio
Ana Reyes

ANDERSON, CHARLES "DOC" (R)

(Sandra) **Waco**
Dist. 56 - McLennan (70%)
Sen. Birdwell

Agriculture & Livestock (VC); Economic & Small Business Development; State and Federal Power and Responsibility

CAPITOL OFFICE
v: 512/463-0135
f: 512/463-0642
GW.8

Staff: Tracy Morehead
Elaine Slaughter

ANDERSON, RODNEY (R)

(Heather) **Grand Prairie**

Dist. 105 - Dallas (7%)

Sens. Hancock, Huffines, West

International Trade & Intergovernmental Affairs; Urban Affairs

CAPITOL OFFICE

v: 512/463-0641
f: 512/463-0044
E1.424

Staff: Jennifer Harris
Jeff Miller
Charnae Stross

ASHBY, TRENT (R)

(Nickie) **Lufkin**

Dist. 57 - Angelina, Houston, Leon, Madison, San Augustine, Trinity

Sens. Nichols, Schwertner

Natural Resources (VC); Appropriations; House Administration

CAPITOL OFFICE

v: 512/463-0508
f: 512/463-5934
E2.414

Staff: Chris Kirby
John Daywalt
Linda Parker

AYCOCK, JIMMIE DON (R)

(Marie) **Killeen**

Dist. 54 - Bell (48%), Lampasas

Sen. Fraser

Public Education (C); *Defense & Veterans' Affairs*

CAPITOL OFFICE

v: 512/463-0684
f: 512/463-8987
E2.708

Staff: Will Holleman
Sam Nancarrow
Lucy Taylor

BELL, JR., CECIL (R)

(Jo Ann) **Magnolia**

Dist. 3 - Montgomery (27%), Waller

Sens. Creighton, Kolkhorst

Appropriations; Land & Resource Management; Rules & Resolutions

CAPITOL OFFICE

v: 512/463-0650
f: 512/463-0575
E2.710

Staff: Jessica Magee
Carolyn Bruton

BERNAL, DIEGO (D)

San Antonio

Dist. 123: Bexar (10%)

Sens. Campbell, Menéndez

International Trade & Intergovernmental Affaris; Urban Affairs

CAPITOL OFFICE

v: 512/463-0532

E2.806
Staff: Leticia Cantu

BLANCO, CÉSAR (D)

El Paso
Dist. 76 - El Paso (20%)
Sen. Rodriguez

Defense & Veterans' Affairs; Public Health; Rules & Resolutions

CAPITOL OFFICE

v: 512/463-0622
f: 512/463-0931
E1.218

Staff: Rebecca Acuna
Larry Porras
Karla Munoz

BOHAC, DWAYNE (R)

(Dawn) **Houston**
Dist. 138 - Harris (4%)
Sens. Bettencourt, Huffman, Whitmire

Public Education; Ways & Means

CAPITOL OFFICE

v: 512/463-0727
f: 512/463-0681
GS.6

Staff: Bradley Pepper
Jeff Stokes
Demeris Burritt

BONNEN, DENNIS H. (R)

(Kim) **Angleton**
Dist. 25 - Brazoria (44%), Matagorda
Sens. Huffman, Kolkhorst, L. Taylor

Ways & Means (C); Natural Resources

CAPITOL OFFICE

v: 512/463-0564
f: 512/463-8414
1W.6

Staff: Shera Eichler
Mitch Carney
Sarah Wolff

BONNEN, M.D., GREG (R)

(Kim) **Friendswood**
Dist. 24 - Galveston (56%)
Sen. L. Taylor

Appropriations; Insurance

CAPITOL OFFICE

v: 512/463-0729
f: 512/463-5896
E2.504

Staff: Brigitt Hartin
Justin Till
Fay Picard

BURKETT, CINDY (R)

(Mike) **Sunnyvale**
Dist. 113 - Dallas (7%)
Sens. Hall, Huffines

Appropriations; Local & Consent Calendars; Transportation

CAPITOL OFFICE

v: 512/463-0464
f: 512/463-9295
E2.322

Staff: Allison Billodeau
Whitney Laning
Carla Pelcastre

BURNS, DEWAYNE (R)

(Jennifer) **Cleburne**
Dist. 58 - Bosque, Johnson
Sen. Birdwell

Homeland Security & Public Safety; Natural Resources

CAPITOL OFFICE

v: 512/463-0538
f: 512/463-0897
E2.804

Staff: Joy Davis
Adrianne Fore
Verlie Edwards

BURROWS, DUSTIN (R)

(Elizabeth) **Lubbock**
Dist. 83 - Borden, Gaines, Lubbock (40%),
Lynn, Mitchell, Scurry, Terry
Sens. Perry, Seliger

County Affairs; International Trade & Intergovernmental Affairs

CAPITOL OFFICE

v: 512/463-0542
f: 512/463-0671
E2.820

Staff: Jeramy Kitchen
Brian Thornton
Daniel Sheppard

BUTTON, ANGIE CHEN (R)

(Darcy) **Garland**
Dist. 112 - Dallas (7%)
Sens. Hall, Huffines, V. Taylor

Economic & Small Business Development (C); Rules & Resolutions;
Ways & Means

CAPITOL OFFICE

v: 512/463-0486
f: 512/463-0793
E2.910

Staff: Amanda Willard
Austin Hood

CANALES, TERRY (D)

(Erica) **Edinburg**
Dist. 40 - Hidalgo (22%)
Sens. Hinojosa, Lucio

Criminal Jurisprudence; Energy Resources

CAPITOL OFFICE

v: 512/463-0426
f: 512/463-0043
E2.816

Staff: Curtis Smith
Alex Rios

CAPRIGLIONE, GIOVANNI (R)

(Elisa) **Southlake**
Dist. 98 - Tarrant (9%)
Sens. Burton, Hancock, Nelson

Appropriations; Investments & Financial Services;
Local & Consent Calendars

CAPITOL OFFICE

v: 512/463-0690
f: 512/463-1004
E2.714

Staff: Amanda Calongne
Katy Aldredge
Courtney Roberts

CLARDY, TRAVIS (R)

(Judy) **Nacogdoches**

Dist. 11 - Cherokee, Nacogdoches, Rusk

Sens. Eltife, Nichols

Local & Consent Calendars (VC); Higher Education; Judiciary & Civil Jurisprudence; State and Federal Power and Responsibility

CAPITOL OFFICE

v: 512/463-0592
f: 512/463-8792
E2.314

Staff: Kelly Barnes
Judd Messer
Jerri Jones

COLEMAN, GARNET (D)

(Angelique) **Houston**

Dist. 147 - Harris (4%)

Sens. Ellis, Garcia, Whitmire

County Affairs (C); Public Health

CAPITOL OFFICE

v: 512/463-0524
f: 512/463-1260
4N.10

Staff: Christopher Walker
Katy Reagan
Angie Gomez

COLLIER, NICOLE (D)

(Gary) **Fort Worth**

Dist. 95 - Tarrant (9%)

Sens. Burton, Hancock

General Investigating & Ethics (VC); Business & Industry; Public Health

CAPITOL OFFICE

v: 512/463-0716
f: 512/463-1516
E2.508

Staff: Jacob Limon
Ann Bailey
Taryn Stoneking

COOK, BYRON C. (R)

(Kay) **Corsicana**

Dist. 8 - Anderson, Freestone, Hill, Navarro

Sens. Birdwell, Nichols, Schwertner

State Affairs (C); Calendars

CAPITOL OFFICE

v: 512/463-0730
f: 512/463-2506
GN.11

Staff: Toni Barcellona
Laramie Stroud
Ashley Ford

CRADDICK, TOM (R)

(Nadine) **Midland**

Dist. 82 - Crane, Dawson, Martin, Midland, Upton

Sens. Perry, Seliger

Energy Resources; State Affairs

CAPITOL OFFICE

v: 512/463-0500
f: 512/463-7722
1W.9

Staff: Kate Huddleston
Susan Wynn

CROWNOVER, MYRA (R)

Denton

Dist. 64 - Denton (25%)

Sens. Estes, Nelson

Public Health (C); Higher Education

CAPITOL OFFICE

v: 512/463-0582
f: 512/463-0471
1N.10

Staff: Miranda Goodsheller
Sharon Dahl

CYRIER, JOHN (R)

(Rachelle) **Lockhart**

Dist. 17: Bastrop, Caldwell, Gonzales, Karnes, Lee

Sens. Kolkhorst, Watson, Zaffirini

Agriculture & Livestock; Land & Resource Management

CAPITOL OFFICE

v: 512/463-0682
f: 512/463-9955
E2.802

Staff: Melissa Nemecek
Alonzo Wood

DALE, TONY (R)

(Mary) **Cedar Park**

Dist. 136 - Williamson (39%)

Sen. Schwertner

Energy Resources; Homeland Security & Public Safety; Local & Consent Calendars

CAPITOL OFFICE

v: 512/463-0696
f: 512/463-9333
E2.904

Staff: Amy Rister Holloway
Greg Bentch
Madeline McLean

DARBY, DREW (R)

(Clarisa) **San Angelo**

Dist. 72 - Coke, Concho, Glasscock, Howard, Irion, Reagan, Runnels, Sterling, Tom Green

Sens. Perry, Seliger

Energy Resources (C); Ways & Means

CAPITOL OFFICE

v: 512/463-0331
f: 512/463-0517
E1.308

Staff: Jason Modglin
Kate Raetz
Cheryl DeCordova

DAVIS, SARAH (R)

(Kent Adams) **West University Place**

Dist. 134 - Harris (4%)

Sens. Ellis, Huffman, Whitmire

Appropriations; Calendars; General Investigating & Ethics; Public Health

CAPITOL OFFICE

v: 512/463-0389
f: 512/463-1374
E2.310

Staff: Hunter Hughes
Catherine Dunn

DAVIS, YVONNE (D)

Dallas
Dist. 111 - Dallas (7%)
Sens. Hancock, West

Redistricting (VC); Ways & Means (VC); Transportation

CAPITOL OFFICE

v: 512/463-0598
f: 512/463-2297
4N.9

Staff: Lemuel Henry Price
Pitria McKinney

DESHOTEL, JOSEPH "JOE" (D)

Beaumont
Dist. 22 - Jefferson (64%)
Sen. Creighton

Land & Resource Management (C); Public Education

CAPITOL OFFICE

v: 512/463-0662
f: 512/463-8381
GW.12

Staff: Christian Manuel
Jacquelyn Savoy
Melissa Quevedo

DUKES, DAWNNA M. (D)

Austin
Dist. 46 - Travis (16%)
Sen. Watson

Culture, Recreation, & Tourism (VC); Emerging Issues In Texas Law Enforcement (VC); Appropriations

CAPITOL OFFICE

v: 512/463-0506
f: 512/463-7864
1W.2

Staff: Pamela McPeters
Morgan Scott
KiYa Moghaddam

DUTTON, JR., HAROLD V. (D)

Houston
Dist. 142 - Harris (4%)
Sens. Creighton, Ellis, Garcia, Whitmire

Juvenile Justice & Family Issues (C); Public Education

CAPITOL OFFICE

v: 512/463-0510
f: 512/463-8333
3N.5

Staff: Tamoria Jones

ELKINS, GARY (R)

(Julie) Houston
Dist. 135 - Harris (4%)
Sens. Bettencourt, Whitmire

Government Transparency & Operation (C); Urban Affairs

CAPITOL OFFICE

v: 512/463-0722
f: 512/463-2331
4N.3

Staff: Debra Clonts
Edith Gibson
Alex Kuehler

FAIRCLOTH, WAYNE (R)

(Cheryl) **Dickinson**

Dist. 23 - Chambers, Galveston (44%)

Sens. Creighton, L. Taylor

Economic & Small Business Development; Rules & Resolutions; Special Purpose Districts

CAPITOL OFFICE

v: 512/463-0502
f: 512/936-4260
E2.812

Staff: Wesley Starnes
Lauren Cottingham

FALLON, PAT (R)

(Susan) **Frisco**

Dist. 106 - Denton (24%)

Sens. Estes, Nelson

Elections; Special Purpose Districts

CAPITOL OFFICE

v: 512/463-0694
f: 512/463-1130
E2.604

Staff: Shannan Sorrell
Nicholas Wat
Andy Forbes

FARIAS, JOE (D)

(Angie) **San Antonio**

Dist. 118 - Bexar (10%)

Sens. Campbell, Uresti, Zaffirini

County Affairs (VC); Defense & Veterans' Affairs

CAPITOL OFFICE

v: 512/463-0714
f: 512/463-1458
4S.4

Staff: Ana Ramon
Kevin Matula
Melissa Huron

FARNEY, MARSHA (R)

(Bryan) **Georgetown**

Dist. 20 - Burnet, Milam, Williamson (22%)

Sens. Fraser, Schwertner

House Administration; Public Education; State Affairs

CAPITOL OFFICE

v: 512/463-0309
f: 512/463-0049
E2.606

Staff: Aaron Gibson
David Glenn

FARRAR, JESSICA (D)

(Marco Sanchez) **Houston**

Dist. 148 - Harris (4%)

Sens. Ellis, Garcia, Whitmire

Judiciary & Civil Jurisprudence (VC); State Affairs

CAPITOL OFFICE

v: 512/463-0620
f: 512/463-0894
1N.8

Staff: Allison Schmitz
Ariana Campos
Cicely Kay

FLETCHER, ALLEN (R)

(Penny) **Tomball**

Dist. 130 - Harris (4%)

Sens. Bettencourt, Kolkhorst

Emerging Issues In Texas Law Enforcement (C); Business & Industry; Transportation

CAPITOL OFFICE

v: 512/463-0661
f: 512/463-4130
GW.4

Staff: Robert Papierz
Sharon Slover

FLYNN, DAN (R)

(Susan) **Van**

Dist. 2 - Hopkins, Hunt, Van Zandt

Sen. Hall

Pensions (C); Investments & Financial Services; Emerging Issues In Texas Law Enforcement

CAPITOL OFFICE

v: 512/463-0880
f: 512/463-2188
GN.7

Staff: David Erinakes
Janice Melton
Kelli Linza

FRANK, JAMES (R)

(Alisha) **Wichita Falls**

Dist. 69 - Archer, Baylor, Clay, Foard, Knox, Wichita

Sens. Estes, Perry

Defense & Veterans' Affairs (VC); Natural Resources

CAPITOL OFFICE

v: 512/463-0534
f: 512/463-8161
E2.304

Staff: Jim Johnson
Megan Titford
Rhonda Poirot

FRULLO, JOHN (R)

(Patti) **Lubbock**

Dist. 84 - Lubbock (60%)

Sen. Perry

Insurance (C); Culture, Recreation, & Tourism

CAPITOL OFFICE

v: 512/463-0676
f: 512/463-0072
E2.608

Staff: Robin MacEwan
Matt Abel
Jordan Schultz

RICK GALINDO (R)

(Valerie) **San Antonio**

Dist. 117 - Bexar (10%)

Sens. Campbell, Menéndez, Uresti

Government Transparency & Operation; Public Education

CAPITOL OFFICE

v: 512/463-0269
f: 512/463-1096
E1.410

Staff: Joey Parr
Fernando Trevino, Jr.
Jacquelyn Kimmey

GEREN, CHARLIE L. (R)

Fort Worth

Dist. 99 - Tarrant (9%)

Sens. Burton, Nelson

House Administration (C); Calendars; Licensing & Administrative Procedures; State Affairs

CAPITOL OFFICE

v: 512/463-0610
f: 512/463-8310
GW.17

Staff: Laura Grable
Robert Armstrong
Payton Spreen

GIDDINGS, HELEN (D)

Dallas

Dist. 109 - Dallas (7%)

Sens. Hall, West

State Affairs (VC); Appropriations; Calendars

CAPITOL OFFICE

v: 512/463-0953
f: 512/463-5887
GW.11

Staff:

GOLDMAN, CRAIG (R)

(Auryn) **Fort Worth**

Dist. 97 - Tarrant (9%)

Sens. Burton, Nelson

Elections (VC); Licensing & Administrative Procedures

CAPITOL OFFICE

v: 512/463-0608
f: 512/463-8342
E2.720

Staff: Amanda Robertson
Leigh Collins
Ainslie Ellis

GONZALES, LARRY (R)

(Marie) **Round Rock**

Dist. 52 - Williamson (39%)

Sen. Schwertner

Appropriations; Government Transparency & Operation; Local & Consent Calendars; Redistricting

CAPITOL OFFICE

v: 512/463-0670
f: 512/463-1469
E2.418

Staff: Chris Sanchez
Amanda Morgan
Jensen DeGroot

GONZÁLEZ, MARY (D)

Clint

Dist. 75 - El Paso (20%)

Sen. Rodriguez

Agriculture & Livestock; Public Education

CAPITOL OFFICE

v: 512/463-0613
f: 512/463-1237
E1.302

Staff: Corinne Chacon
Genevieve Cato
Joshua Carter

GUERRA, ROBERT (D)

(Leslie) **McAllen**

Dist. 41 - Hidalgo (22%)

Sens. Hinojosa, Lucio

Insurance; Local & Consent Calendars; Public Health

CAPITOL OFFICE

v: 512/463-0578
f: 512/463-1482
E2.818

Staff: Anne Drescher
Aisa Showery
Dahlia Perez

GUILLEN, RYAN (D)

(Dalinda) **Rio Grande City**

Dist. 31 - Atascosa, Brooks, Duval, Jim Hogg, Kenedy, LaSalle, Live Oak, McMullen, Starr, Willacy

Sens. Hinojosa, Lucio, Uresti, Zaffirini

Culture, Recreation, & Tourism (C); Licensing & Administrative Procedures

CAPITOL OFFICE

v: 512/463-0416
f: 512/463-1012
4S.3

Staff: Robert M. McVey
Ben Wright
Rebecca Donachie

GUTIERREZ, ROLAND (D)

(Sarah) **San Antonio**

Dist. 119 - Bexar (9%)

Sens. Campbell, Menéndez, Uresti

Licensing & Administrative Procedures (VC); Government Transparency & Operation; Local & Consent Calendars

CAPITOL OFFICE

v: 512/463-0452
f: 512/463-1447
GN.9

Staff: Margaret Frain
Wallace

HARLESS, PATRICIA F. (R)

(Sam) **Spring**

Dist. 126 - Harris (4%)

Sens. Bettencourt, Whitmire

Calendars; State Affairs; Transportation

CAPITOL OFFICE

v: 512/463-0496
f: 512/463-1507
E2.408

Staff: Julie Scott
Staci Rives
Laurel Burrin

HERNANDEZ, ANA (D)

Houston

Dist. 143 - Harris (4%)

Sens. Garcia, Whitmire

Judiciary & Civil Jurisprudence; Pensions

CAPITOL OFFICE

v: 512/463-0614
f: 512/463-0612
4S.2

Staff: Maria Delgado
Matthew Hall
Linda Jamail

HERRERO, ABEL (D)

(Matilda) **Robstown**

Dist. 34 - Nueces (51%)

Sen. Hinojosa

Criminal Jurisprudence (C); *Energy Resources*

CAPITOL OFFICE

v: 512/463-0462
f: 512/463-1705
GW.6

Staff: Jesus Moreno
Azra Siddigi
Matilda Saenz

HOWARD, DONNA (D)

(Derek) **Austin**

Dist. 48 - Travis (17%)

Sens. Campbell, Watson, Zaffirini

Higher Education (VC); *Appropriations*; *House Administration*

CAPITOL OFFICE

v: 512/463-0631
f: 512/463-0901
E1.420

Staff: Scott Daigle
Jacob Cottingham
Stella Savage

HUBERTY, DAN (R)

(Janet) **Houston**

Dist. 127 - Harris (4%)

Sens. Bettencourt, Creighton, Whitmire

Calendars; *Public Education*; *State Affairs*

CAPITOL OFFICE

v: 512/463-0520
f: 512/463-1606
E2.722

Staff: Casey Christman
Ben Melson
Molly Spratt

HUGHES, BRYAN (R)

Mineola

Dist. 5 - Camp, Morris, Rains, Smith (24%) Titus, Wood

Sens. Eltife, Hall

Appropriations; *Juvenile Justice & Family Issues*

CAPITOL OFFICE

v: 512/463-0271
f: 512/463-1515
4S.5

Staff: Cody Terry

HUNTER, TODD (R)

(Alexis) **Corpus Christi**

Dist. 32 - Nueces (49%)

Sens. Hinojosa, Kolkhorst

Calendars (C); *Urban Affairs (VC)*; *Criminal Jurisprudence*; *General Investigating & Ethics*; *Redistricting*

CAPITOL OFFICE

v: 512/463-0672
f: 512/463-2101
GW.18

Staff: Caleb McGee
Angie Flores
Dan Leyendecker

REPRESENTATIVES

ISAAC, JASON A. (R)

(Carrie) **Dripping Springs**

Dist. 45 - Blanco, Hays

Sens. Campbell, Fraser, Zaffirini

Economic & Small Business Development; Environmental Regulation; Local & Consent Calendars

CAPITOL OFFICE

v: 512/463-0647
f: 512/463-3573
E1.414

Staff: G. Michael Brown
Chelsey McGee
Carrie Nelson

ISRAEL, CELIA (D)

Austin

Dist. 50 - Travis (16%)

Sen. Watson

Elections; Transportation

CAPITOL OFFICE

v: 512/463-0821
f: 512/463-1199
E1.406

Staff: Jennie Kennedy
Kathryn Garza

JOHNSON, ERIC (D)

(Nakita) **Dallas**

Dist. 100 - Dallas (7%)

Sens. Hall, West

Economic & Small Business Development (VC); Calendars; Homeland Security & Public Safety

CAPITOL OFFICE

v: 512/463-0586
f: 512/463-8147
E1.204

Staff: Conor Kenny
Kerry Goodwin
Ocie Kazee-McCallister

KACAL, KYLE J. (R)

(Marci) **College Station**

Dist. 12 - Brazos (16%), Falls, Limestone, McLennan (30%), Robertson

Sens. Birdwell, Schwertner

Rules & Resolutions (VC); Environmental Regulation; Natural Resources

CAPITOL OFFICE

v: 512/463-0412
f: 512/463-0412
E2.420

Staff: Terra Willett
Ryan Skrobarczyk
Julian Whitley

KEFFER, JAMES L. "JIM" (R)

(Leslie) **Eastland**

Dist. 60 - Brown, Callahan, Coleman, Eastland, Hood, Palo Pinto, Shackelford, Stephens

Sens. Birdwell, Estes, Fraser, Perry

Natural Resources (C); Energy Resources; Redistricting

CAPITOL OFFICE

v: 512/463-0656
f: 512/478-8805
1W.11

Staff: Adam Haynes
Tori Regas
Greer Gregory

KEOUGH, MARK (R)

(Kimberly) **The Woodlands**
Dist. 15 - Montgomery (37%)
Sen. Creighton

Corrections; Human Services

CAPITOL OFFICE

v: 512/463-0797
f: 512/463-0898
E2.402

Staff: Jason Millsaps
Kurt Jones
Ruth Mesta

KING, KEN (R)

(Robin) **Canadian**
Dist. 88 - Armstrong, Bailey, Briscoe, Castro,
Cochran, Donley, Gray, Hale, Hansford,Hemphill,
Hockley, Lamb, Lipscomb, Ochiltree, Roberts,
Swisher, Yoakum
Sens. Perry, Seliger

Calendars; Environmental Regulation; House Administration;
Public Education

CAPITOL OFFICE

v: 512/463-0736
f: 512/463-0211
E2.416

Staff: Cheryl Lively
Megan Quijano
Amber Hunter

KING, PHIL S. (R)

(Terry) **Weatherford**
Dist. 61 - Parker, Wise
Sen. Estes

State and Federal Power and Responsibility (C); *Energy Resources;*
Environmental Regulation

CAPITOL OFFICE

v: 512/463-0738
f: 512/463-1957
1N.5

Staff: Ashley Westenhover
Judy Flanagin

KING, SUSAN LEWIS (R)

(Austin) **Abilene**
Dist. 71 - Jones, Nolan, Taylor
Sens. Fraser, Perry

Defense & Veterans' Affairs (C); *Human Services*

CAPITOL OFFICE

v: 512/463-0718
f: 512/463-0994
GN.12

Staff: Bryan W. Law
Kolby Monnig
Cooper McLendon

KING, TRACY O. (D)

(Cheryl) **Batesville**
Dist. 80 - Dimmit, Frio, Uvalde,
Webb (36%), Zapata, Zavala
Sens. Uresti, Zaffirini

Agriculture & Livestock (C); *Natural Resources*

CAPITOL OFFICE

v: 512/463-0194
f: 512/463-1220
GW.7

Staff: Celina Overbo
Sam Bacarisse

KLICK, STEPHANIE (R)

(Don) **Fort Worth**
Dist. 91 - Tarrant (9%)
Sens. Burton, Hancock

Human Services; Pensions

CAPITOL OFFICE

v: 512/463-0599
f: 512/463-0751
E2.716

Staff: Bryan Shufelt
Amber Ray
Steven Will

KOOP, LINDA (R)

Dallas
Dist. 102 - Dallas (7%)
Sens. Huffines, V. Taylor

Appropriations; International Trade & Intergovernmental Affairs; Emerging Issues In Texas Law Enforcement

CAPITOL OFFICE

v: 512/463-0454
f: 512/463-1121
E1.512

Staff: Ryan Sparks
Candace Carver
Ashley Mann

KRAUSE, MATT (R)

(Jennie) **Fort Worth**
Dist. 93 - Tarrant (9%)
Sens. Burton, Hancock, Nelson

Corrections; Land & Resource Management

CAPITOL OFFICE

v: 512/463-0562
f: 512/463-2053
E2.212

Staff: Clayton Knippa
Edward Jaax
Scott Stier

KUEMPEL, JOHN (R)

(Michelle) **Seguin**
Dist. 44 - Guadalupe, Wilson
Sens. Campbell, Zaffirini

General Investigating & Ethics (C); Licensing & Administrative Procedures; State Affairs

CAPITOL OFFICE

v: 512/463-0602
f: 512/480-0391
E2.422

Staff: Brittney Madden
Thomas Flanders
Angela Avila

LANDGRAF, BROOKS (R)

(Shelby) **Odessa**
Dist. 81 - Andrews, Ector, Ward, Winkler
Sens. Perry, Seliger

Energy Resources; Investments & Financial Services

CAPITOL OFFICE

v: 512/463-0546
f: 512/463-8067
E1.312

Staff: Michael Lozano
Marshall Bowen

LARSON, LYLE (R)

San Antonio
Dist. 122 - Bexar (10%)
Sens. Campbell, Menéndez, Uresti

Calendars; Culture, Recreation, & Tourism; General Investigating & Ethics; Natural Resources

CAPITOL OFFICE

v: 512/463-0646
f: 512/463-0893
E2.406

Staff: Lynlie Wallace
Shannon Houston

LAUBENBERG, JODIE (R)

(Bob) **Parker**
Dist. 89 - Collin (22%)
Sens. Estes, V. Taylor

Elections (C); Judiciary & Civil Jurisprudence

CAPITOL OFFICE

v: 512/463-0186

1N.7

Staff: Suzanne Bowers
Brett Sebastian
Helen Hansen

LEACH, JEFF (R)

(Becky) **Plano**
Dist. 67 - Collin (22%)
Sen. V. Taylor

Criminal Jurisprudence; Government Transparency & Operation

CAPITOL OFFICE

v: 512/463-0544
f: 512/463-9974
E1.314

Staff: Mary McClure
Creighton Root

LONGORIA, OSCAR (D)

(Jennifer) **Mission**
Dist. 35 - Cameron (17%), Hidalgo (13%)
Sens. Hinojosa, Lucio

Investments & Financial Services (VC); Appropriations

CAPITOL OFFICE

v: 512/463-0645
f: 512/463-0559
E1.510

Staff: Lee Loya
Michelle Villarreal
Tony Flores, Jr.

LOZANO, J.M. (R)

(Abby) **Kingsville**
Dist. 43 - Bee, Jim Wells, Kleberg, San Patricio
Sens. Hinojosa, Lucio, Zaffirini

Redistricting (C); International Trade & Intergovernmental Affairs (VC); Environmental Regulation

CAPITOL OFFICE

v: 512/463-0463
f: 512/463-1765
E2.908

Staff: Matt Lamon

LUCIO III, EDDIE (D)

(Jaime) **Brownsville**
Dist. 38 - Cameron (41%)
Sen. Lucio

Calendars (VC); Land & Resource Management; Natural Resources

CAPITOL OFFICE

v: 512/463-0606
f: 512/463-0660
E1.320

Staff: Ruben O'Bell
Houston Tower

MÁRQUEZ, MARISA (D)

(Francisco Martinez) **El Paso**
Dist. 77 - El Paso (20%)
Sen. Rodriguez

House Administration (VC); Appropriations; Culture, Recreation, & Tourism; Emerging Issues In Texas Law Enforcement

CAPITOL OFFICE

v: 512/463-0638
f: 512/463-8908
E2.822

Staff: Chasity Tillis
Bryce Romero
Amanda Saucedo

MARTINEZ, ARMANDO A. (D)

(Marisa) **Weslaco**
Dist. 39 - Hidalgo (22%)
Sen. Lucio

Transportation (VC); Higher Education; Emerging Issues In Texas Law Enforcement

CAPITOL OFFICE

v: 512/463-0530
f: 512/463-0849
4N.4

Staff: Scott Jenkins
Paco Sanchez
Magaly Torres

MARTINEZ FISCHER, TREY (D)

(Elizabeth Provencio) **San Antonio**
Dist. 116 - Bexar (10%)
Sens. Menéndez, Uresti

Special Purpose Districts; Ways & Means

CAPITOL OFFICE

v: 512/463-0616
f: 512/463-4873
1W.3

Staff: Summer Luciano
Alison Ross

MCCLENDON, RUTH JONES (D)

(Denver) **San Antonio**
Dist. 120 - Bexar (10%)
Sens. Campbell, Menéndez, Urest

Rules & Resolutions (C); Appropriations; Transportation

CAPITOL OFFICE

v: 512/463-0708
f: 512/463-7071
3S.2

Staff: Janis Reinken
Linda Christofilis
Marge Reyna

METCALF, WILL (R)

(Megan) **Conroe**
Dist. 16 - Montgomery (37%)
Sens. Creighton, Nichols

Economic & Small Business Development;
Homeland Security & Public Safety

CAPITOL OFFICE

v: 512/463-0726
f: 512/463-8428
E2.704

Staff: Seth Juergens
Frank Fenlaw
Guadalupe Cuellar

MEYER, MORGAN (R)

(Keana) **Dallas**
Dist. 108 - Dallas (7%)
Sens. Hall, Huffines, West

Energy Resources; Insurance

CAPITOL OFFICE

v: 512/463-0367
f: 512/322-9935
E1.418

Staff: Matt Creel
Sallie Armstrong
Shelby Goff

MILES, BORRIS L. (D)

(Cydonii) **Houston**
Dist. 146 - Harris (4%)
Sens. Ellis, Huffman

Appropriations; Licensing & Administrative Procedures; State and Federal
Power and Responsibility

CAPITOL OFFICE

v: 512/463-0518
f: 512/463-0941
E2.718

Staff: Shalette Mitchell
Camille Foster
J. Clayton Riley

MILLER, DOUG (R)

(Anne) **New Braunfels**
Dist. 73 - Comal, Gillespie, Kendall
Sens. Campbell, Fraser

Special Purpose Districts (C); *Licensing & Administrative Procedures*

CAPITOL OFFICE

v: 512/463-0325
f: 512/463-6161
GN.10

Staff: Tammy Pirtle
Hayley Budden
Flo Sultemeier

MILLER, RICK (R)

(Babs) **Sugar Land**
Dist. 26 - Fort Bend (27%)
Sens. Huffman, Kolkhorst

Appropriations; Public Health

CAPITOL OFFICE

v: 512/463-0710
f: 512/463-0711
E2.312

Staff: Courtney Hjaltman
Margaret Reiney
Jason Kirksey

REPRESENTATIVES

MOODY, JOE (D)

(Adrianne) **El Paso**
Dist. 78 - El Paso (20%)
Sen. Rodriguez

Criminal Jurisprudence (VC); General Investigating & Ethics; Homeland Security & Public Safety

CAPITOL OFFICE
v: 512/463-0728
f: 512/463-0397
E2.214

Staff: Ellic Sahualla
Jen Shugert
Ana Gonzalez

MORRISON, GEANIE W. (R)

(Jack) **Victoria**
Dist. 30 - Aransas, Calhoun, DeWitt, Goliad, Refugio, Victoria
Sen. Kolkhorst

Environmental Regulation (C); Higher Education

CAPITOL OFFICE
v: 512/463-0456
f: 512/463-0158
1N.9

Staff: Justin Unruh
James Zafereo

MUÑOZ, JR., SERGIO (D)

(Maria Elena) **Palmview**
Dist. 36 - Hidalgo (22%)
Sens. Hinojosa, Lucio

Insurance (VC); Appropriations; Local & Consent Calendars

CAPITOL OFFICE
v: 512/463-0704
f: 512/463-5364
E1.508

Staff: Dylan Matthews
Loradel Mariano
Peter Salinas

MURPHY, JIM (R)

(Kathleen) **Houston**
Dist. 133 - Harris (4%)
Sens. Bettencourt, Huffman, Whitmire

Corrections (C); Ways & Means

CAPITOL OFFICE
v: 512/463-0514
f: 512/463-8715
E1.408

Staff: Martha Bell Liner
Deanna Harrington
Benjamin Williams

MURR, ANDREW (R)

(Lacey) **Junction**
Dist. 53 - Bandera, Crockett, Edwards, Kerr, Kimble, Llano, Mason, Medina, Menard, Real, Schleicher, Sutton
Sens. Fraser, Perry, Uresti

Culture, Recreation, & Tourism; Rules & Resolutions; Transportation

CAPITOL OFFICE
v: 512/463-0536
f: 512/463-1449
E1.412

Staff: Regan Ellmer
Debra Van Bibber
Brooke Bohlen

REPRESENTATIVES

NAISHTAT, ELLIOTT (D)

Austin
Dist. 49 - Travis (16%)
Sens. Watson, Zaffirini

Public Health (VC); Human Services

CAPITOL OFFICE
v: 512/463-0668

GW.16
Staff: Judith Dale
Jessica Boston
Dorothy Browne

NEVÁREZ, PONCHO (D)

(Rossy) **Eagle Pass**
Dist. 74 - Brewster, Culberson, Hudspeth, Jeff Davis, Kinney, Loving, Maverick, Pecos, Presidio, Reeves, Terrell, Val Verde
Sens. Rodriguez, Seliger, Uresti

Homeland Security & Public Safety (VC); Local & Consent Calendars; Natural Resources

CAPITOL OFFICE
v: 512/463-0566
f: 512/463-0220
E1.306
Staff: Oberlyn Salinas
Lauren Cacheaux
Caitlyn Ashley

OLIVEIRA, RENÉ O. (D)

Brownsville
Dist. 37 - Cameron (42%)
Sen. Lucio

Business & Industry (C); Redistricting; State Affairs

CAPITOL OFFICE
v: 512/463-0640
f: 512/463-8186
3N.6
Staff: J.J. Garza
Tony Gray
Angelina Lopez

OTTO, JOHN C. (R)

(Nancy) **Dayton**
Dist. 18 - Liberty, San Jacinto, Walker
Sens. Nichols, Schwertner

Appropriations (C)

CAPITOL OFFICE
v: 512/463-0570
f: 512/463-0315
E1.504
Staff: Nikki Cobb
Ryan Ambrose
Melva Gomez

PADDIE, CHRIS (R)

(Brooke) **Marshall**
Dist. 9 - Cass, Harrison, Marion, Panola, Sabine, Shelby
Sens. Eltife, Nichols

Energy Resources (VC); House Administration; Transportation

CAPITOL OFFICE
v: 512/463-0556
f: 512/463-0611
E2.412
Staff: John Buxie
Ray Wilson

PARKER, TAN (R)

(Beth) **Flower Mound**
Dist. 63 - Denton (25%)
Sen. Nelson

Investments & Financial Services (C); Redistricting; State and Federal Power and Responsibility; Ways & Means

CAPITOL OFFICE

v: 512/463-0688
f: 512/480-0694
E2.602

Staff: Richard Dennis
Jordan Taylor
Eric Viining

PAUL, DENNIS (R)

(Eliza) **Houston**
Dist. 129 - Harris (4%)
Sens. Garcia, L. Taylor

Insurance; Pensions

CAPITOL OFFICE

v: 512/463-0734
f: 512/463-0401
E2.814

Staff: Mitzi C. Stoute
Cristian Perez
Debra Risinger

PEÑA, GILBERT (R)

(Cynthia) **Pasadena**
Dist. 144 - Harris (4%)
Sens. Garcia, L. Taylor

Human Services; Juvenile Justice & Family Issues

CAPITOL OFFICE

v: 512/463-0460
f: 512/463-0763
E1.416

Staff: Maricela De Leon
Mikael A. Garcia

PHELAN, DADE (R)

(Kim) **Port Neches**
Dist. 21 - Jefferson (36%), Orange
Sens. Creighton, Nichols

Appropriations; Elections

CAPITOL OFFICE

v: 512/463-0706
f: 512/463-1861
E1.324

Staff Zach Johnson
Lauren Lumsden
Gatlin Moncla

PHILLIPS, LARRY (R)

(Robin) **Sherman**
Dist. 62 - Delta, Fannin, Grayson
Sens. Estes, Hall

Homeland Security & Public Safety (C); Transportation

CAPITOL OFFICE

v: 512/463-0297
f: 512/463-1561
4N.5

Staff: Sara Haenes
Chris Tarter

PICKETT, JOSEPH C. "JOE" (D)

(Shannon) **El Paso**

Dist. 79 - El Paso (20%)

Sen. Rodriguez

Transportation (C); Investments & Financial Services; Redistricting

CAPITOL OFFICE

v: 512/463-0596
f: 512/463-6504
1W.5

Staff: Michael Breitinger
Sam Gammage
Jill Breitinger

PRICE, FOUR (R)

(Karen) **Amarillo**

Dist. 87 - Carson, Hutchison, Moore, Potter, Sherman

Sen. Seliger

Appropriations; Calendars; Human Services

CAPITOL OFFICE

v: 512/463-0470
f: 512/463-8003
E2.610

Staff: Hal Talton
Cailey McLain
Sandra Talton

RANEY, JOHN (R)

(Elizabeth) **Bryan**

Dist. 14 - Brazos (84%)

Sen. Schwertner

Appropriations; Higher Education; House Administration

CAPITOL OFFICE

v: 512/463-0698
f: 512/463-5109
E2.706

Staff: Anna Hynes
Austin McCarty
Leo Mathers

RAYMOND, RICHARD PEÑA (D)

(Michelle) **Laredo**

Dist. 42 - Webb (64%)

Sen. Zaffirini

Human Services (C); Judiciary & Civil Jurisprudence

CAPITOL OFFICE

v: 512/463-0558
f: 512/463-6296
1W.4

Staff: David Leo
Abigail Martinez
Jim Terrell

REYNOLDS, RON (D)

(Jonita) **Missouri City**

Dist. 27 - Fort Bend (27%)

Sens. Ellis, Huffman

Elections; Environmental Regulation

CAPITOL OFFICE

v: 512/463-0494
f: 512/463-1403
E2.306

Staff: Jennifer Brader
Glen Smith

RIDDLE, DEBBIE (R)

(Mike) **Tomball**
Dist. 150 - Harris (4%)
Sens. Bettencourt, Creighton

Juvenile Justice & Family Issues (VC); Calendars; Energy Resources

CAPITOL OFFICE
v: 512/463-0572
f: 512/463-1908
4N.7

Staff: Shelton Green
Gail Gallien

RINALDI, MATT (R)

(Corely) **Irving**
Dist. 115 - Dallas (7%)
Sen. Huffines

Agriculture & Livestock; Business & Industry

CAPITOL OFFICE
v: 512/463-0468
f: 512/463-1044
E1.422

Staff: Desiree Smith
Sal Ayala
Stewart McGregor

RODRIGUEZ, EDDIE (D)

(Christine) **Austin**
Dist. 51 - Travis (17%)
Sens. Watson, Zaffirini

Environmental Regulation (VC); Calendars; Economic & Small Business Development

CAPITOL OFFICE
v: 512/463-0674
f: 512/463-0314
4S.6

Staff: Laura S. Hoke
Deisy A. Jaimes
Huey Rey Fischer

RODRIGUEZ, JUSTIN (D)

(Victoria) **San Antonio**
Dist. 125 - Bexar (10%)
Sens. Menéndez, Uresti

Appropriations; Pensions; Rules & Resolutions

CAPITOL OFFICE
v: 512/463-0669
f: 512/463-5074
E1.212

Staff: Brian Hodgdon
Jessalyn Reid
Cynthia Chapa

ROMERO, JR., RAMON (D)

Fort Worth
Dist. 90 - Tarrant (9%)
Sens. Burton, Hancock, Nelson

Business & Industry; County Affairs

CAPITOL OFFICE
v: 512/463-0740
f: 512/463-1075
E1.208

Staff: Leo Aguirre
Michael Ramsey

ROSE, TONI (D)

Dallas
Dist. 110 - Dallas (7%)
Sens. Hall, West

Human Services (VC); Juvenile Justice & Family Issues; Rules & Resolutions

CAPITOL OFFICE

v: 512/463-0664
f: 512/463-0476
E2.302

Staff: Trevin Franklin
Lauren Gray

SANFORD, SCOTT (R)

(Shelly) **McKinney**
Dist. 70 - Collin (22%)
Sens. Estes, V. Taylor

Juvenile Justice & Family Issues; Land & Resource Management

CAPITOL OFFICE

v: 512/463-0356
f: 512/463-0701
E2.210

Staff: Katherine Munal
Megan Pulley

SCHAEFER, MATT (R)

(Jasilyn) **Tyler**
Dist. 6 - Smith (76%)
Sen. Eltife

Defense & Veterans' Affairs; Urban Affairs

CAPITOL OFFICE

v: 512/463-0584
f: 512/463-3217
E2.510

Staff: Judd Quarles
Alisha Jackson
Jack Short

SCHOFIELD, MIKE (R)

Katy
Dist. 132 - Harris (4%)
Sens. Bettencourt, Huffman, Kolkhorst

Elections; Judiciary & Civil Jurisprudence

CAPITOL OFFICE

v: 512/463-0528
f: 512/463-7820
E2.316

Staff: Rachel Nicholson
Deandra Porter

SCHUBERT, LEIGHTON (R)

(Brittany) **Caldwell**
Dist. 13: Austin, Burleson, Colorado,
Fayette, Grimes, Lavaca, Washington
Sens.: Kolkhorst, Schwertner

Corrections, County Affairs

CAPITOL OFFICE

v: 512/463-0600
f: 512/463-5240
E2.208

Staff: Manny Salazar

SHAHEEN, MATT (R)

(Robyn) **Plano**

Dist. 66 - Collin (22%)

Sen. V. Taylor

Criminal Jurisprudence; Defense & Veterans' Affairs

CAPITOL OFFICE

v: 512/463-0594
f: 512/463-1021
E1.322

Staff: Christopher Paxton
Kevin Goldsmith
William Gray

SHEETS, KENNETH (R)

(Michele) **Dallas**

Dist. 107 - Dallas (7%)

Sens. Hall, Huffines

Insurance; Judiciary & Civil Jurisprudence; Local & Consent Calendars

CAPITOL OFFICE

v: 512/463-0244
f: 512/463-9967
E1.404

Staff: Dustin Meador
Casey Bingham
Mackenzie Oliphant

SHEFFIELD, J.D. (R)

Gatesville

Dist. 59 - Comanche, Coryell, Erath, Hamilton, McCulloch, Mills, San Saba, Somervell

Sens. Birdwell, Estes, Fraser, Perry

Appropriations; Public Health; Rules & Resolutions

CAPITOL OFFICE

v: 512/463-0628
f: 512/463-3644
E2.320

Staff: Andrew Johnson
Amanda Kit Tollett
Gary Kafer

SIMMONS, RON (R)

(Lisa) **Carrollton**

Dist. 65 - Denton (25%)

Sen. Nelson

Business & Industry (VC); Transportation

CAPITOL OFFICE

v: 512/463-0478
f: 512/463-2089
E2.712

Staff: Ben Lancaster
Ebony Daughtry
Zach Flores

SIMPSON, DAVID (R)

(Susan) **Longview**

Dist. 7 - Gregg, Upshur

Sen. Eltife

Agriculture & Livestock; Criminal Jurisprudence

CAPITOL OFFICE

v: 512/463-0750
f: 512/463-9085
E2.502

Staff: Kathi Seay
Michael Bullock
Emily Nicholson

REPRESENTATIVES

SMITH, WAYNE (R)

(Brenda) **Baytown**

Dist. 128 - Harris (4%)

Sens. Creighton, L. Taylor, Garcia, Whitmire,

Licensing & Administrative Procedures (C);
Culture, Recreation, & Tourism

CAPITOL OFFICE

v: 512/463-0733
f: 512/463-1323
GN.8

Staff: Amanda Schar
Jessica Effenberger
Murphy McCollough

SMITHEE, JOHN T. (R)

(Becky) **Amarillo**

Dist. 86 - Dallam, Deaf Smith, Hartley, Oldham, Parmer, Randall

Sen. Seliger

Judiciary & Civil Jurisprudence (C); State Affairs

CAPITOL OFFICE

v: 512/463-0702
f: 512/476-7016
1W.10

Staff: Andrea Stingley
Beth Klunder
Elin Isenhower

SPITZER, M.D., STUART (R)

(Shari) **Kaufman**

Dist. 4 - Henderson (83%), Kaufman

Sens. Hall, Nichols

County Affairs; Human Services

CAPITOL OFFICE

v: 512/463-0458
f: 512/463-2040
E1.316

Staff: Robert Shulter
Matt Sims
Reagan Moreland

SPRINGER, JR., DREW (R)

(Lydia) **Muenster**

Dist. 68 - Childress, Collingsworth, Cooke, Cottle, Crosby, Dickens, Fisher, Floyd, Garza, Hall, Harde-man, Haskell, Jack, Kent, King, Montague, Motley, Stonewall, Throckmorton, Wheeler, Wilbarger, Young

Sens. Estes, Perry, Seliger

Agriculture & Livestock; Local & Consent Calendars; Ways & Means

CAPITOL OFFICE

v: 512/463-0526
f: 512/463-1011
E2.410

Staff: Jonathan Mathers
Mark Thorne
Jennifer Vogel

STEPHENSON, PHIL (R)

(Barbara) **Wharton**

Dist. 85 - Fort Bend (18%), Jackson, Wharton

Sens. Huffman, Kolkhorst

Investments & Financial Services; Pensions

CAPITOL OFFICE

v: 512/463-0604
f: 512/463-5244
E2.906

Staff: Matt Minor
Hope Ruiz
Kate McWhorter

STICKLAND, JONATHAN (R)

(Krystal) **Bedford**
Dist. 92 - Tarrant (9%)
Sens. Burton, Hancock, Nelson

County Affairs; Special Purpose Districts

CAPITOL OFFICE
v: 512/463-0522
f: 512/463-9529
E1.402

Staff: Tim Hardin
Nicole Paulette
Murphy Simpson

STRAUS III, JOE (R)

(Julie) **San Antonio**
Dist. 121 - Bexar (10%)
Sens. Campbell, Menéndez

Speaker of the House of Representatives

CAPITOL OFFICE
v: 512/463-1000
f: 512/463-0675
2W.13

Staff: Jesse Ancira
Patricia Shipton
Andrew Blifford

THOMPSON, ED (R)

(Freddie) **Pearland**
Dist. 29 - Brazoria (56%)
Sen. L. Taylor

Land & Resource Management (VC); Environmental Regulation

CAPITOL OFFICE
v: 512/463-0707
f: 512/463-8717
E2.506

Staff: Emily Kirchner
Grace Richardson
Madison Sachanowicz

THOMPSON, SENFRONIA (D)

Houston
Dist. 141 - Harris (4%)
Sens. Bettencourt, Ellis, Garcia, Whitmire

Local & Consent Calendars (C); *Judiciary & Civil Jurisprudence;*
Licensing & Administrative Procedures; Redistricting

CAPITOL OFFICE
v: 512/463-0720
f: 512/463-6306
3S.6

Staff: Milda Mora
Brete Anderson
Colleen Tran

TINDERHOLT, TONY (R)

(Bethany) **Fort Worth**
Dist. 94 - Tarrant (9%)
Sens. Birdwell, Burton, Hancock

Corrections; County Affairs

CAPITOL OFFICE
v: 512/463-0624
f: 512/463-8386
E1.216

Staff: Micah Cavanaugh
Allison Ngo
Jake Robinson

TURNER, CHRIS (D)

(Lisa) **Grand Prairie**

Dist. 101 - Tarrant (9%)

Sens. Birdwell, Burton, Hancock

General Investigating & Ethics; Higher Education; Ways & Means

CAPITOL OFFICE

v: 512/463-0574
f: 512/463-1481
E2.318

Staff: Emily Amps
Devan Allen
Any Callahan

TURNER, SCOTT (R)

(Robin) **Rockwall**

Dist. 33 - Collin (12%), Rockwall

Sens. Estes, Hall, V. Taylor

Government Transparency & Operation; International Trade & Intergovernmental Affairs

CAPITOL OFFICE

v: 512/463-0484
f: 512/463-7834
E1.318

Staff: Deanna Kuykendall
Justin Stone
Thomas DiJiuseppe

TURNER, SYLVESTER (D)

Houston

Dist. 139 - Harris (4%)

Sens. Garcia, Whitmire

Appropriations (VC); State Affairs

CAPITOL OFFICE

v: 512/463-0554
f: 512/463-8380
GW.15

Staff: Alison Brock
Murry Matthews
Pamela Watson

VANDEAVER, GARY (R)

(Pam) **New Boston**

Dist. 1 - Bowie, Franklin, Lamar, Red River

Sen. Eltife

Appropriations; Public Education

CAPITOL OFFICE

v: 512/463-0692
f: 512/463-0902
E1.310

Staff: Trish Conradt
Madison Stewart

VILLALBA, JASON (R)

(Brooke) **Dallas**

Dist. 114 - Dallas (7%)

Sens. Hall, Huffines, V. Taylor

Business & Industry; Economic & Small Business Development

CAPITOL OFFICE

v: 512/463-0576
f: 512/463-7827
E2.404

Staff: Ashley Juergens
Michael Blair
Christine Mojezati

VO, HUBERT (D)

(Kathy) **Houston**

Dist. 149 - Harris (4%)

Sens. Ellis, Huffman

Economic & Small Business Development; House Administration; Insurance

CAPITOL OFFICE

v: 512/463-0568
f: 512/463-0548
4N.8

Staff: Tanya Walker
Matthew Lemin
Karen Loper

WALLE, ARMANDO L. (D)

(Debbie) **Houston**

Dist. 140 - Harris (4%)

Sens. Garcia, Whitmire

*Government Transparency & Operation (VC); Appropriations;
State and Federal Power and Responsibility*

CAPITOL OFFICE

v: 512/463-0924
f: 512/463-1510
E1.304

Staff: Rahul Sreenivasan
Myriam Saldivar
Raul Lopez

WHITE, JAMES (R)

Hillister

Dist. 19 - Hardin, Jasper, Newton, Polk, Tyler

Sen. Nichols

*Corrections (VC); Juvenile Justice & Family Issues;
Emerging Issues In Texas Law Enforcement*

CAPITOL OFFICE

v: 512/463-0490
f: 512/463-9059
E2.204

Staff: Jonathan Covey
Saul Mendoza
Natalie Smith

WHITE, MOLLY S. (R)

(Ronald) **Belton**

Dist. 55 - Bell (52%)

Sen. Fraser

Homeland Security & Public Safety; Urban Affairs

CAPITOL OFFICE

v: 512/463-0630
f: 512/463-0937
E2.702

Staff: Hannah Bell
Trent Williams

WORKMAN, PAUL D. (R)

(Sherry) **Austin**

Dist. 47 - Travis (17%)

Sens. Campbell, Fraser, Watson

*State and Federal Power and Responsibility (VC); Insurance;
Natural Resources*

CAPITOL OFFICE

v: 512/463-0652
f: 512/463-0565
E2.902

Staff: Don Barber
Blake Rogers
Brian Mitchell

WRAY, JOHN (R)

(Michele) **Waxahachie**

Dist. 10 - Ellis, Henderson (17%)

Sens. Birdwell, Nichols

Homeland Security & Public Safety; Ways & Means

CAPITOL OFFICE

v: 512/463-0516
f: 512/463-1051
E1.220

Staff: Tabatha Vasquez
Daniel Mittnacht
David Turner

WU, GENE (D)

(Miya Shay) **Houston**

Dist. 137 - Harris (4%)

Sens. Ellis, Huffman

County Affairs; Energy Resources

CAPITOL OFFICE

v: 512/463-0492
f: 512/463-1182
E2.810

Staff: Amy Bruno
Beth Martin
Greg Wythe

ZEDLER, WILLIAM "BILL" (R)

(Ellen) **Arlington**

Dist. 96 - Tarrant (9%)

Sens. Birdwell, Burton

Public Health; Special Purpose Districts

CAPITOL OFFICE

v: 512/463-0374
f: 512/463-0364
GS.2

Staff: Matthew Posey
Charlotte Blakemore

ZERWAS, M.D., JOHN (R)

Richmond

Dist. 28 - Fort Bend (27%)

Sens. Huffman, Kolkhorst

Higher Education (C); Public Health

CAPITOL OFFICE

v: 512/463-0657
f: 512/236-0713
E2.308

Staff: Nelda Hunter
Cameron Cocke
Kelley Mathis

District 124

Special Election Pending

Dist. 124 - Bexar (10%)

Sens. Uresti, Menéndez

State Affairs; Transportation

CAPITOL OFFICE

v: 512/463-0634
f:
Room

Staff:

HOUSE STANDING COMMITTEES

Hon. Joe Straus III, *Speaker of the House*   Hon. Dennis Bonnen, *Speaker Pro Tem*

AGRICULTURE & LIVESTOCK
Clerk: Sam Bacarisse   E2.114 • 512/463-0762

T. King, *Chair*   C. Anderson, *Vice Chair*

Members: Cyrier,González, Rinaldi, Simpson, Springer

APPROPRIATIONS
Clerk: Jonathon Storms   E1.032 • 512/463-1091 / Fax: 463-0270

Otto, *Chair*   Sylvester Turner, *Vice Chair*

Members: Ashby, Bell, G. Bonnen, Burkett, Capriglione, S. Davis, Dukes, Giddings, Gonzales, Howard, Hughes, Koop, Longoria, Márquez, McClendon, Miles, R. Miller, Muñoz, Phelan, Price, Raney, J. Rodriguez, Sheffield, VanDeaver, Walle

BUSINESS & INDUSTRY
Clerk: Angelina Lopez   E2.128 • 512/463-0766 / Fax: 463-8186

Oliveira, *Chair*   Simmons, *Vice Chair*

Members: Collier, Fletcher, Rinaldi, Romero, Villalba

CALENDARS
Clerk: Ginny Bell   E2.148 • 512/463-0758

Hunter, *Chair*   Lucio, *Vice Chair*

Members: Alonzo, Cook, S. Davis, Geren, Giddings, Harless, Huberty, Johnson, K. King, Larson, Price, Riddle, E. Rodriguez

CORRECTIONS
Clerk: Laurie McAnally   E2.110 • 512/463-0796

Murphy, *Chair*   J. White, *Vice Chair*

Members: Allen, Keough, Krause, Schubert, Tinderholt

COUNTY AFFAIRS
Clerk: Katy Reagan   E2.130 • 512/463-0760 / Fax: 463-5227

Coleman, *Chair*   Farias, *Vice Chair*

Members: Burrows, Romero, Schubert, Spitzer, Stickland, Tinderholt, Wu

CRIMINAL JURISPRUDENCE
Clerk: Miguel Liscano   E2.112 • 512/463-0768

Herrero, *Chair*   Moody, *Vice Chair*

Members: Canales, Hunter, Leach, Shaheen, Simpson

CULTURE, RECREATION, & TOURISM
Clerk: Rebecca Donachie   E2.134 • 512/463-1974 / Fax: 463-0237

Guillen, *Chair*   Dukes, *Vice Chair*

Members: Frullo, Larson, Márquez, Murr, Smith

HOUSE STANDING COMMITTEES

DEFENSE & VETERANS' AFFAIRS
Clerk: Tracy Winston   E2.160 • 512/463-1393 / Fax: 463-1023
S. King, *Chair*   Frank, *Vice Chair*
Members: Aycock, Blanco, Farias, Schaefer, Shaheen

ECONOMIC & SMALL BUSINESS DEVELOPMENT
Clerk: Victoria Smith   E2.118 • 512/463-0069
Button, *Chair*   Johnson, *Vice Chair*
Members: C. Anderson, Faircloth, Isaac, Metcalf, E. Rodriguez, Villalba, Vo

ELECTIONS
Clerk: Katharine Chambers   E2.144 • 512/463-0772
Laubenberg, *Chair*   Goldman, *Vice Chair*
Members: Fallon, Israel, Phelan, Reynolds, Schofield

ENERGY RESOURCES
Clerk: Jamie Burchfield   E2.162 • 512/463-0774
Darby, *Chair*   Paddie, *Vice Chair*
Members: Anchia, Canales, Craddick, Dale, Herrero, Keffer, P. King, Landgraf, Meyer, Riddle, Wu

ENVIRONMENTAL REGULATION
Clerk: James Zafereo   E2.154 • 512/463-0776 / Fax: 463-9503
Morrison, *Chair*   E. Rodriguez, *Vice Chair*
Members: Isaac, Kacal, K. King, P. King, Lozano, Reynolds, E. Thompson

GENERAL INVESTIGATING & ETHICS
Clerk: Brittney Madden E2.170 • 512/463-0780
Kuempel, *Chair*   Collier, *Vice Chair*
Members: S. Davis, Hunter, Larson, Moody, C. Turner

GOVERNMENT TRANSPARENCY & OPERATION
Clerk: Teri Avery   E2.206 • 512/463-0903
Elkins, *Chair*   Walle, *Vice Chair*
Members: Galindo, Gonzales, Gutierrez, Leach, Scott Turner

HIGHER EDUCATION
Clerk: Cameron Cocke E2.106 • 512/463-0782
Zerwas, *Chair*   Howard, *Vice Chair*
Members: Alonzo, Clardy, Crownover, Martinez, Morrison, Raney, C. Turner

HOUSE STANDING COMMITTEES

HOMELAND SECURITY & PUBLIC SAFETY
Clerk: Courtney Reid   E2.146 • 512/463-0133

Phillips, *Chair*   Nevarez, *Vice Chair*

Members: Burns, Dale, Johnson, Metcalf, Moody, M. White, Wray

HOUSE ADMINISTRATION
Clerk: Laura Grable   E2.140/GW17 • 512/463-0784 / Fax: 463-8310

Geren, *Chair*   Márquez, *Vice Chair*

Members: Allen, Alonzo, Ashby, Farney, Howard, K. King, Paddie, Raney, Vo

HUMAN SERVICES
Clerk: Jim Terrell   E2.152 • 512/463-0786 / Fax: 463-8981

Raymond, *Chair*   Rose, *Vice Chair*

Members: Keough, S. King, Klick, Naishtat, Pena, Price, Spitzer

INSURANCE
Clerk: Jesse Sifuentez E2.150 • 512/463-0788 / Fax: 476-7016

Frullo, *Chair*   Muñoz, *Vice Chair*

Members: G. Bonnen, Guerra, Meyer, Paul, Sheets, Vo, Workman

INTERNATIONAL TRADE & INTERGOVERNMENTAL AFFAIRS
Clerk: Jeff Madden   E2.158 • 512/463-1211

Anchia, *Chair*   Lozano, *Vice Chair*

Members: R. Anderson, Bernal, Burrows, Koop, Scott Turner

INVESTMENTS & FINANCIAL SERVICES
Clerk: Julie Young   E2.172 • 512/463-0871

Parker, *Chair*   Longoria, *Vice Chair*

Members: Capriglione, Flynn, Landgraf, Pickett, Stephenson

JUDICIARY & CIVIL JURISPRUDENCE
Clerk: Beth Klunder   E2.120 • 512/463-0790 / Fax: 463-0174

Smithee, *Chair*   Farrar, *Vice Chair*

Members: Clardy, Hernandez, Laubenberg, Raymond, Schofield, Sheets, S. Thompson

JUVENILE JUSTICE & FAMILY ISSUES
Clerk: Tamoria Jones   E2.202 • 512/463-0794

Dutton, *Chair*   Riddle, *Vice Chair*

Members: Hughes, Peña, Rose, Sanford, J. White

LAND & RESOURCE MANAGEMENT
Clerk: Melissa Quevedo E2.136 • 512/463-1623 / Fax: 463-8342

Deshotel, *Chair*   E. Thompson, *Vice Chair*

Members: Bell, Cyrier, Krause, Lucio, Sanford

HOUSE STANDING COMMITTEES

LICENSING & ADMINISTRATIVE PROCEDURES
Clerk: Gabe Valenzuela E2.156 • 512/463-0798

Smith, *Chair*   Gutierrez, *Vice Chair*

Members: Geren, Goldman, Guillen, Kuempel, Miles, D. Miller, S. Thompson

LOCAL & CONSENT CALENDARS
Clerk: Milda Mora   E2.166 • 512/463-0800

S. Thompson, *Chair*   Clardy, *Vice Chair*

Members: Burkett, Capriglione, Dale, Gonzales, Guerra, Gutierrez, Isaac, Muñoz, Nevarez, Sheets, Springer

NATURAL RESOURCES
Clerk: Buffy Barrett   E2.104 • 512/463-0802

Keffer, *Chair*   Ashby, *Vice Chair*

Members: Bonnen, Burns, Frank, Kacal, T. King, Larson, Lucio, Nevarez, Workman

PENSIONS
Clerk: Andrew Graham E2.164 • 512/463-2054 / Fax: 463-3083

Flynn, *Chair*   Alonzo, *Vice Chair*

Members: Hernandez, Klick, Paul, J. Rodriguez, Stephenson

PUBLIC EDUCATION
Clerk: Ryan Marquess   E2.124 • 512/463-0804

Aycock, *Chair*   Allen, *Vice Chair*

Members: Bohac, Deshotel, Dutton, Farney, Galindo, González, Huberty, K. King, VanDeaver

PUBLIC HEALTH
Clerk: Rudy England   E2.1010 • 512/463-0806 / Fax: 463-0900
Crownover, *Chair*   Naishtat, *Vice Chair*

Members: Blanco, Coleman, Collier, S. Davis, Guerra, R. Miller, Sheffield, Zedler, Zerwas

REDISTRICTING
Clerk: Grady Dahlberg E2.142 • 512/463-9948

Lozano, *Chair*   Y. Davis, *Vice Chair*

Members: Gonzales, Hunter, Keffer, Oliveira, Parker, Pickett, S. Thompson

RULES & RESOLUTIONS
Clerk: Linda Christofilis E2.138 • 512/463-0812

McClendon, *Chair*   Kacal, *Vice Chair*

Members: Alvarado, Bell, Blanco, Button, Faircloth, Murr, J. Rodriguez, Rose, Sheffield

HOUSE STANDING COMMITTEES

SPECIAL PURPOSE DISTRICTS
Clerk: Elizabeth Fazio   E2.1016 • 512/463-0277 / Fax: 463-0977

D. Miller, *Chair*   Alvarado, *Vice Chair*

Members: Faircloth, Fallon, Martinez Fischer, Stickland, Zedler

STATE AFFAIRS
Clerk: Toni Barcellona   E2.108 • 512/463-0814 / Fax: 463-6783

Cook, *Chair*   Giddings, *Vice Chair*

Members: Craddick, Farney, Farrar, Geren, Harless, Huberty, Kuempel, Oliveira, Smithee, Sylvester Turner, Dist. 124

TRANSPORTATION
Clerk: Sam Gammage   E2.122 • 512/463-0818 / Fax: 463-1469

Pickett, *Chair*   Martinez, *Vice Chair*

Members: Burkett, Y. Davis, Fletcher, Harless, Israel, McClendon, Murr, Paddie, Phillips, Simmons, Dist. 124

URBAN AFFAIRS
Clerk: E2.126 • 512/463-9904 / Fax: 463-1049

Alvarado, *Chair*   Hunter, *Vice Chair*

Members: R. Anderson, Bernal, Elkins, Schaefer, M. White

WAYS & MEANS
Clerk: Jennifer Rabb   E2.116 • 512/463-0822 / Fax: 463-1529

Bonnen, *Chair*   Y. Davis, *Vice Chair*

Members: Bohac, Button, Darby, Martinez Fischer, Murphy, Parker, Springer, C. Turner, Wray

SELECT COMMITTEE ON EMERGING ISSUES IN TEXAS LAW ENFORCEMENT
Clerk: Sherri Walker   JHR 311, 512/463-8160

Fletcher, *Chair*   Dukes, *Vice Chair*

Members: Flynn, Koop, Márquez, Martinez, J. White

SELECT COMMITTEE ON STATE AND FEDERAL POWER AND RESPONSIBILITY
Clerk: Aaron Whitehead   JHR 312, 512/463-8159

P. King, *Chair*   Workman, *Vice Chair*

Members: C. Anderson, Clardy, Miles, Parker, Walle

STEPS IN THE LEGISLATIVE PROCESS

This diagram displays the sequential flow of a bill from the time it is introduced in the house of representatives to final passage and transmittal to the Governor. A bill introduced in the senate would follow the same procedure in reverse.

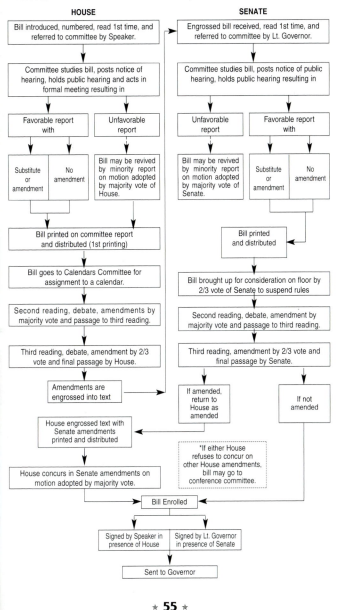

HOUSE SEATING CHART

VILLALBA	DALE	GONZALES		PENA	DIST. 124	KEFFER	MURPHY
ANCHIA		VANDEAVER		ISRAEL	HOWARD	DESHOTEL	SIMPSON
C. TURNER		WU		BLANCO	VO	M. WHITE	SCHAEFER
LUCIO		HERNANDEZ		K. KING	DUTTON	TINDERHOLT	STICKLAND
LONGORIA		ROSE		KUEMPEL	FRUILO	BURROWS	MILES
MARQUEZ		S. DAVIS		FARNEY	PADDIE	GIDDINGS	SYL. TURNER
GALINDO		WRAY		PRICE	LARSON	ALLEN	FARRAR
METCALF		KACAL		CRADDICK	PARKER	MOODY	MARTINEZ
CLARDY		ASHBY		DARBY	AYCOCK	SANFORD	KRAUSE
STEPHENSON		PHELAN		ZERWAS	CROWNOVER	DUKES	MCCLENDON

Y. DAVIS	ALONZO	MORRISON	RANEY
REYNOLDS	CAPRIGLIONE	P. KING	BURKETT
FRANK	ISAAC	HUGHES	J. WHITE

SPEAKER
JOE

HUBERTY	KLICK	MARTINEZ FISCHER	HUNTER	COOK	PHILLIPS
FAIRCLOTH	GUTIERREZ	NEVAREZ	GONZALEZ	COLEMAN	HERRERO
KEOUGH	BURNS	COLLIER	J. RODRIGUEZ	FARIAS	WALLE
S. KING	NAISHTAT	SHEFFIELD	KOOP	SIMMONS	SPRINGER
E RODRIGUEZ	MEYER	MURR	LANDGRAF	GOLDMAN	G. BONNEN
OLIVEIRA	CANALES	SPITZER	R. ANDERSON	LEACH	E. THOMPSON
SCHUBERT	CYRIER	RINALDI	FALLON	LAUBENBERG	SHEETS
WORKMAN	PAUL	SCHOFIELD	SHAHEEN	SCOTT TURNER	BELL
RIDDLE	R. MILLER	BOHAC	FLETCHER	T. KING	ELKINS
S. THOMPSON	D. ANDERSON	GUERRA	ROMERO	ZEDLER	FLYNN

HOUSE
S III

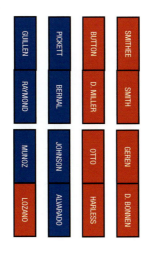

GUILLEN | PICKETT | BUTTON | SMITHEE
RAYMOND | BERNAL | D. MILLER | SMITH
MUNOZ | JOHNSON | OTTO | GEREN
LOZANO | ALVARADO | HARLESS | D. BONNEN

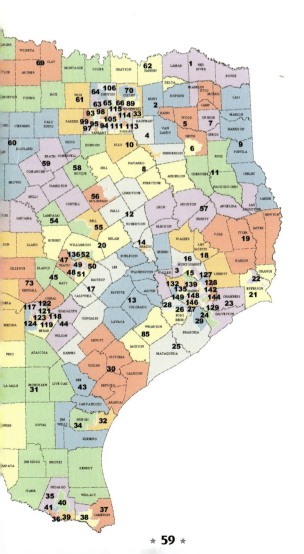

HOTELS   AUSTIN

AT&T Executive Education and Conference Center	512/404-1900
Driskill Hotel	512/474-5911
Four Seasons Hotel	512/478-4500
Hotel Ella	512/495-1800
Hyatt Regency Austin	512/477-1234
InterContinental Stephen F. Austin	512/457-8800
Omni Austin Hotel	512/476-3700
Renaissance Austin	512/343-2626
Sheraton Austin at the Capitol	512/478-1111
W Austin Hotel	512/542-3600

RESTAURANTS

III Forks	512/474-1776
Austin Land & Cattle Co	512/472-1813
Bob's Steak & Chop House	512/222-BOBS
Carmelo's Ristorante Italiano	512/477-7497
Cisco's	512/478-2420
Fogo de Chão Brazilian Steakhouse	512/472-0220
Lonesome Dove Western Bistro	www.cheftimlove.com
Matt's El Rancho	512/462-9333
Perry's Steakhouse and Grille	512/474-6300
Ranch 616	512/479-7616
Rattle Inn	512/373-8306

CLUBS

Austin Club	512/477-9496
Headliners Club	512/479-8080
The University of Texas Club	512/477-5800

RENT-A-CAR

Alamo/National (ABIA)	512/476-6189
Avis (ABIA)	512/530-3400
Budget (ABIA)	512/530-3350
Enterprise	888/291-0359
Hertz (ABIA)	512/530-3600

TAXICAB

Austin Cab	512/478-2222
Yellow Cab	512/452-9999

AIRLINES

American Airlines	800/433-7300
Delta Airlines	800/221-1212
Jet Blue Airways	800/538-2583
Southwest Airlines	800/435-9792
US Airways/AA	800/433-7300
United Airlines	800/241-6522

7